FOOTNOTES

FOOTNOTES

A collection of scripts devised by
Footprints Theatre Company

edited by
Steve & Janet Stickley

HODDER AND STOUGHTON
LONDON   SYDNEY   AUCKLAND   TORONTO

British Library Cataloguing in Publication Data

Footnotes: a collection of scripts devised
   by Footprints Theatre Company.
   1. Christian Life—Drama
   I. Stickley, Steve   II. Stickley, Janet
   III. Footprints Theatre Company
   248.4   BV4501.2

   ISBN 0-340-40579-1

To Ronald Mann for showing us the fulfilment of Joel 2:28 in his own life, an inspiring combination of age and youth:

... your old men will dream dreams, your young men will see visions.

ACKNOWLEDGMENTS

Our very grateful thanks to all the members of Footprints Theatre Company whose love, energy, inspiration and valued friendship over the years have helped to shape an exciting vision. Quite simply, without them our work and therefore this book would not exist. Credit must go to the following nine people who, together with us, formed the Company between 1978 and 1984: including Robin Crawford, Rachel Goodman, Nigel and Lizzie Styles, Chris Humble, Louise Skeat and Mark Estdale; and special recognition of the rôle played by Philip Hawthorn and Alan MacDonald in the creation of much of the material to be found in this book.

Thanks also to Colin Dawson, Ronald Mann, Lance Pierson, Barbara Ramsden, Mark Stickley and, of course, Sally Hennessy for struggling with an often stubborn typewriter.

S & J Stickley

LICENCE TO PERFORM THE SKETCHES IN THIS VOLUME

ABBREVIATIONS OF STAGE DIRECTIONS

CS	Centre stage	OSL	Offstage left
DS	Downstage	OSR	Offstage right
DSC	Downstage centre	SL	Stage left
DSL	Downstage left	SR	Stage right
DSR	Downstage right	US	Upstage
MSL	Midstage left	USC	Upstage centre
MSR	Midstage right	USL	Upstage left
OS	Offstage	USR	Upstage right

CONTENTS

INTRODUCTION   13

PRACTICAL SESSIONS   17

SECTION 1   WORSHIP

   i Family   Nasty Zac   27
                     Be a Hero   40
                     RSVP   53
                     Signs and Blunders   56
                     A Ripping Time   67

   ii Adult   Wodger Say?   88
                     Quenching the Thirst   94
                     God-sand   96
                     Churchopoly   100
                     Spitlight   107
                     For Form's Sake   113
                     One Body   119

SECTION 2   MUSICAL

        Mr G   124
        Pedestals   143
        Introducing that Jaunting
            Jackanapes . . . Jonah!   147

SECTION 3   FAST, FURIOUS AND THOUGHTFUL

   i Shorter pieces   Plane Sailing   155
                                 Action Replay   172

                    Bad Noose, Good Noose   178
                    My Way   190
                    Dirty Rag   198
                    The Lost Coin   209

ii One Act Play   About Face   215
                    Notes on making masks   235

BIBLIOGRAPHY   240

INTRODUCTION

Authors often have the irksome habit of adding a footnote to the text just when you didn't want the flow interrupted – particularly when you have only just started reading the book.* Drama can have that same irritating habit of making you notice things which you might otherwise have easily overlooked. It interrupts the flow and makes people sit up and take notice. As Christians, the irritant which our drama can provide in people's lives may act like a grain of sand in an oyster, eventually producing a beautiful pearl of great price, but first we have to dive for the oysters and that is where the real hard work comes in. Good drama requires commitment as well as enthusiasm and *Footnotes* is designed to help you whether your group is just beginning or wanting to grow together in experience.

The pieces of drama in this book have been drawn from a repertoire of plays and sketches by Footprints Theatre Company which has developed over a period of several years. There is not room here to publish the many one-act plays written by the company since 1978 which have formed the back-bone of its work, but we have included a comprehensive selection of shorter pieces which have proved very useful and effective.

Much of this material has grown from improvisation with a group of actors rather than from the pen of one or two writers. As a result a style has emerged which owes its character as much to the physical dimension as to the verbal. Reading through the collection you will often find copious directions for action and mime, also suggestions for

* See what we mean?

the use of vocal sound effects – both originally the result of improvisational exercises and experiments. With this in mind your preparation for performing most of the pieces, whether you are in a group who work regularly together or not, should concentrate firmly on the physical angle in order to stimulate your actors, teach them physical discipline and to prepare them for what is to come. This is especially relevant for the following pieces included in this book: 'Nasty Zac', 'A Ripping Time', 'Mr G', 'Bad Noose, Good Noose', 'My Way' and 'Dirty Rag'. Such preparation is absolutely vital for 'Plane Sailing' and 'About Face'.

Work like this should be done through workshop sessions such as the one outlined on page 18. A workshop like this should provide a useful springboard into the text, hopefully producing greater insight in group members than if the very first approach was, 'Let's pick up this script and see what we can do with it.' If the preparation for the workshop is done carefully and confidently you may find that some of the ideas that result may even be usable for a drama of your own. In the end, you will derive greater satisfaction and fulfilment from this approach than simply relying on a script that is presented on a plate with all the thinking done for you. The book of drama material you are holding in your hand should feed and supplement your group's creativity, not replace it.

We hope your group's own interpretation, or style, will eventually develop from exploring and performing these (and other) pieces. Beware of the consumer attitude prevalent among some Christian drama groups which says, 'Great! Another load of sketches for us to use and use and use until they're done to death.' Perhaps there ought to be a health warning down the spine of this book, reading, 'Misuse of this source material can lead to stunted creativity and a very narrow outlook.' If you are a group eager to perform, great! But remember, you are people with gifts and talents (we hope!) that need to be nurtured and encouraged. Part of the Christian's calling to proclaim the message to the world is to attend very carefully not only to what you say, but also to the way you say it; not just what you show, but also the way you show it. Don't use drama exclusively to 'grab people for the Gospel', but learn to see that through the process of understanding, interpreting and presenting it there is much to learn about yourself, your group and your God.

Actor, Ego and God

'In drama, we have to face the fact that for an actor to be good, he needs to have an inherent desire to glorify himself.' If this objection voiced by the British Evangelical Council Study Group on the use of television (August 1981) is true, then all is lost. As a group of trained, experienced actors and committed Christians, members of Footprints over the years have discovered and rediscovered that the actor should, in fact, be a servant. This is important because it gives a balanced view, recognising that the talent to act is accountable to the one who gave the talent in the first place.

When an actor bows to an audience he is not, as is popularly believed, taking the glory for himself. (Although this could often be the case!) Rather, it *should* be the action of one who has 'given' a play to an audience; he has served the audience and the playwright by enabling the written word to become flesh. He gives away his performance, his art, so that others may respond, reflect and learn. He bows as a servant bows before his master after performing some service for him. The actor who has an inherent desire to glorify himself, is, we believe, a bad actor. The attention should be on the play, not the player. Following on from this then, if the creative gifts are handled and channelled correctly, the play itself should ultimately draw our attention to the giver, not to the gift. And the only appropriate footnote to that must be 'Amen'!

Steve and Janet Stickley
NOTTINGHAM 1986

PRACTICAL SESSIONS

The first of the following sessions is an absolute *must* if you want your group to get under the skin of many of the scripts in this book. You will find the time spent actually on your feet doing the practical exercises here will prove a wise investment when it comes to picking up a script from the next section.

It is advisable for one person to lead these workshops in order to instil some discipline from the word go. There is also something quite exciting for those taking part if they have no idea what is coming next, so keep these plans up your sleeve and put the group through their paces (they only really need to appreciate the very basic reason for doing it). The surprise value in a workshop such as this is always useful; people's imaginations can be so easily stultified or quenched by long explanations of what is going to happen next and why. Let them work it out as you go along and then talk about it afterwards.

A final word before you launch into this practical work: make sure you are familiar with the workshop plan. Reread it and make your own notes. Be sure you understand it. Don't have this book open in front of you when you are leading the session – in fact you could lock yourself in your bedroom for a couple of hours and almost learn the different exercises, if you think your brain is up to it! Either way a notebook will be invaluable as you will see.

Note: You may decide that a Saturday morning or after-noon would be a good time for these workshops. Weekday evenings tend to find people half asleep or seized-up after about nine o'clock. So unless any of you are ardent football fans or Tesco till-ringers a Saturday should mean you are a more alert and lively troupe!

Busy Bodies and Brains

Aim: To nurture a physical awareness and involvement within the group and to stimulate further dramatic ideas.

1 *Warm-up Games*
   These are designed to be enjoyed but they also help members to break down barriers and relax.
   i *My Bonny*. Stand in a circle and sing together the first verse and chorus of 'My Bonny lies over the ocean', making sure those who don't know it have time to pick it up. On every word beginning with B perform a simple action, e.g. thumbs start off in an upward position at arm's length. On a word starting with B rotate them to a downward position. On the next B word rotate them back up and so on. Then extend this to arms in the air, arms down, arms back up, and so on. It is surprisingly difficult not to make a mistake. Increase speed. (You can invent your own actions if you play it often.)   10 minutes

   ii *Rocks and Snakes*. All but one of the group form an interlocking firm structure which will be the 'rock'. This can be achieved by some on hands and knees, others bending over, some crouching down or across other group members, etc. The 'rock' must provide a fairly stable structure. The 'snake' now writhes and wriggles through the big and small holes created by the interlocking people, exploring every conceivable entrance and exit. Repeat a couple of times with different people as the 'snake'. (Removal of jewellery and belts with buckles is advised.)   10 minutes

2 *Drama Exercises*

These should foster an understanding that the whole body may be used to communicate something specific. Encourage an increase of concentration during the machines section.

i *Alphabet*

(a) Each person stands alone facing away from the others. Someone shouts out letters from the alphabet at random. Everyone must make the shape of the capital letter using the whole body and endeavouring to keep the letters vertical. The pace must quicken considerably. Encourage everyone to think it out for themselves. 5 minutes

(b) Experiment with spelling words using the actors as the individual letters. If there are enough of you, split up into groups of three and devise a message of three three-lettered words and see if the rest can read it. Otherwise send one person out of the room, taking it in turns to guess. 10 minutes

ii *Machines*

In twos think of a household gadget or machine with working parts. Each pair constructs the machine employing their whole bodies. Care should be given to create the shape, how it operates and is operated, e.g. a person's thumb could become a switch to activate a large foodmixer – person two providing the beating action with arms in a bowl-shaped configuration of legs! Suitable vocal noises should be encouraged to help bring the whole thing to life. The rest of the group attempt to operate the machines in turn and see if they can guess its function. Compare notes and repeat using different partners and a different category, e.g. an amusement arcade, a railway station, etc.

20 minutes

3 *Story Building*

This stage is crucial in order to help group members see how this all ties in with performance.

i *Nursery Rhymes*

(a) Depending upon your group number split into twos or threes. Each group secretly selects a nursery rhyme (or draws choices randomly to ensure they have different rhymes). The actors then devise a way of re-telling the story using only physical expression and vocal sound effects – no words at all. Encourage groups to employ their whole bodies once more and to exercise imagination, e.g. one person could be a tuffet which then turns into a spider. Or two people could form a spider together, they should invent noises to help convey the atmosphere; perhaps the spider may issue a guttural threatening noise while the curds and whey slop and drip, etc. Scope should be given for the actors to become anything at all, animate or inanimate.   10 minutes

(b) Arrange for the pairs, or threes, to join with another pair to perform their stories for each other to see if they can guess the respective rhymes. Each then gives constructive advice on how to improve the stories. A critical eye should be fostered, e.g. 'I didn't know you were a spider, maybe you could try a more darting quality of movement', etc. Five more minutes are given to work on them again incorporating the advice.   20 minutes

(c) All the stories are performed for everyone. Briefly discuss the impact, difficulties, entertainment value, etc.   15–20 minutes

(A cup of coffee wouldn't go amiss here!)

ii *Skeletal Story*

Still in twos or threes read out the following:

There is a rich person who works very hard and becomes even richer. He turns very self-satisfied and proud. Suddenly he dies. There is a mysterious scene that takes place after his death.

At this stage no mention should be given to the remarkable resemblance of this story to Luke 12:16–20!

Your group then give this the same treatment as the nursery rhymes except that they are permitted to use a few onomatopoeic words as punctuation, e.g. 'splash', 'lunge', 'grab', 'pat', 'kapow!', etc. Give them all the opportunity to flesh out the bare bones of the story just how they want. It can be set anywhere, any time, as long as they adhere to the storyline. The same process as in the nursery rhyme section is followed.

40–50 minutes

It is important that these timings are enforced. The pressure of working against the clock actually helps individuals to think as they experiment rather than think *then* experiment. The evaluations in discussion times are invaluable but control is needed to prevent their turning into long exegeses.

This second workshop could be used with the group sometime later to develop insights into character-based drama ideas.

Of Mice and Men

Aim: To encourage an understanding of the possible development of a character and to broaden the group's imaginative scope and potential for building characters and dramatic situations.

1 *Warm-up Games*
   Both of these will help to develop quick thinking, concentration and group spirit.
   i *Category Tig*   A simple chasing game. Decide on a

category (in this instance *animals*) and designate one person to be 'on' or 'it'. The catcher pursues the others and tries to touch them. Those being chased must think of the name of an animal and when they are approached by the catcher they may stop, crouch, touch the floor and shout as loud as they can the name of the animal, e.g. zebra, mole, iguana, or whatever. This effectively prevents them from being caught. No animal must be repeated – anyone who does so becomes the catcher. The pace should accelerate to breakneck speed, speaking figuratively of course. (Other categories may be used on other occasions for general warm-ups, such as: British prime ministers, makes of car, recipes, newspapers and journals, and so on.)   5–10 minutes

ii *Chief Pig*   The group sits in a circle of chairs. One is designated Chief Pig. Everyone is given an animal identity around the circle, one at a time until you reach the last person (sitting next to Chief Pig) who becomes the lowest of the low – the Worm. Each is given a suitable noise and action. Chief Pig: two nasal snorts with hands as trotters tucked under chin. Rabbit: 'Nibble nibble' with hands on head for ears. Sheep: 'Baa' with both hands spiralling down from the ears to show wool. Crocodile: 'Snap. Snap' with arms outstretched forward like huge jaws and hands slapping together. Skunk: 'Phaw' holding nose with one hand and wafting an imaginary odour with the other, etc. (Invent your own according to number, or even personality.) Lastly the Worm: 'Eee. Eee' with one finger wiggling up in the air. There will be some hilarity as these are briefly practised ready for the game. The aim is for everyone to unseat Chief Pig and occupy his/her position themselves.

Chief Pig starts by making his own noise and action immediately followed by that of one of the other animals in the circle, e.g. the Crocodile. The Crocodile then responds by first snapping his 'jaws' and then doing the noise and action of another animal, e.g. the Rabbit, who then makes his own nibbling gesticulation then another's and so on. You are not allowed to pass back the noise-action to the animal who sent it to you (unless you are playing with less than five people); if you do or if you make any other mistake (wrong noise with action, etc.) you must vacate your seat and become the miserable Worm at the bottom. All those animals between you and the Worm move up one seat towards Chief Pig. When this happens each person who has moved *changes* animal identity to that originally owned by the occupier of the *seat*. No discussion is permitted. The game should get faster and more furious, and a rhythm should emerge as each person becomes more competent – unfortunately the mirth often incurred renders some people more *in*competent as the game progresses. Great fun.   15–20 minutes

2 *Drama Exercises*

  i Remaining in the circle initiate a brief discussion which concentrates on analysing and describing the characteristics of certain animals – you could talk about some used in the game. Encourage group members to think of descriptive words, especially those that describe the movements. Break out of circle, putting chairs away.
      5–10 minutes

  ii Very quickly go through a few limbering-up exercises to mobilise neck, shoulders, back, hips, etc. 3 minutes

  iii Each person sits on the floor with eyes shut. (Your verbal instructions during this next section are very important; they need to command concentration and encourage imagination. Without your playing the tyrant, it must be made clear that they do what you say and stop when you say stop.) Ask them to imagine an animal, preferably one not previously used in 'Chief Pig'. Get them to think about the qualities of its movements, and encourage them to start moving around the room experimenting with these characteristics. Stop them and sit down as before.

Now emphasise that they are going to translate those qualities into human movements rather than animal ones. Repeat the exercise to develop a human character with animal-like characteristics. This time when you stop, get them to 'freeze' in whatever position they are in and ask them to think about what sort of clothing this character would wear. Give them a little longer to move around to develop their ideas.

Stop and repeat all the above process using a different animal. This time, towards the end encourage them to decrease the movements so they become more natural and less absurd. Try going one stage further and get them to develop a voice. This can be easily accomplished by telling them to answer a ringing telephone on a given signal (if they all speak simultaneously it helps to overcome any self-consciousness).   20 minutes

3 *Improvisations*
   i Discuss what you have been doing, extending the discussion into people you know or famous people and the type of animal with which you might equate them.
                    5–10 minutes

   ii Go back to individual work. Start off as for *2 ii*, this time allowing each person to choose his own animal. Take the development a lot further, encouraging him to decide on a name, what his living room looks like (get him to move around it picking up imaginary objects, etc.), what sort of interests he has, and so on. Then bring them together in character and hold brief conversations on a given topic such as a topical news item; eventually take them back to their living rooms. Give them a short time to think through the way of their development.   15 minutes iii With you in a role yourself (e.g. a police person), call a meeting for the group to attend, sustaining their respective characters. Initiate a group discussion (e.g. a neighbourhood scheme to prevent burglaries) and see what happens. Draw out any shy characters and control the more verbose. After about 10 minutes break this and see if people can guess the animals from which others' characters were derived.   15 minutes

iv. Discuss the process of translating animal attributes to human ones and whether they stood the test of credibility. Talk about any problems encountered.
                                                                    5 minutes

4 *Story Building*
This last section could go in a variety of directions, but if you want to develop an idea for a performance piece based on a Bible story or parable, then take your chosen passage, read it and talk about (a) what type of 'animals' the characters involved could be and (b) where it could all take place, etc., and take notes ready for another session. (See page 36ff in *Using the Bible in Drama* by the authors.)   20 minutes

If you want to continue to explore the group's original ideas further, spend 10 minutes creating new characters and put them into different situations in twos – meeting on a beach at midnight, both accidentally locked in a supermarket, at breakfast in a hotel where a crime has been committed the night before – and see what the outcome is. Talk about the work you have just done, adjusting your planning to incorporate everyone's thought and ideas. Jot down any particularly striking moments.   30 minutes

Bear in mind that this is only one way of exploring character building. Encourage the group to observe people in the coming week. Compare notes on intriguing conversations, chance meetings, people who have made you laugh/scared you/embarrassed you, etc. For plot and situations collect newspaper cuttings, personal experiences and imaginary possibilities (you could play a type of 'consequences' where actors are required to become characters in situations drawn from a hat). The benefits of doing more of this exploratory work from the point of view of expanding a group's resources and firing the imagination can be immense.

You may want to extend work like this into further practical sessions. There are many useful books that give guidelines for improvisation. (See Bibliography and also consult your local library.) *Using the Bible in Drama* by the authors and Jim Belben (Bible Society) and *Move Yourselves* by Gordon and Ronni Lamont (also Bible Society) provide detailed help. Always scribble down in your notebook the ideas that come during these times and also look out for people's gifts that may emerge: comic timing, ability to show emotion, a strong sense of rhythm, unusual and original ideas, etc. All such strengths should be nurtured and channelled into either devising your own dramas and/or interpreting set scripts.

SECTION 1 – WORSHIP

i Family

NASTY ZAC

This short play has proved immensely popular with junior-age children and family audiences. Always a good starter it helps to diffuse a possibly starchy church congregation and leaves a relaxed sense of well-being. (If it doesn't then you've missed something vital.) A participatory song with actions is an ideal follower to this; perhaps one about how good God is, or Jesus as a special friend. There is a lot of scope for extra improvised comments in the piece, but the actors must be relaxed and very familiar with it. Despite that, don't allow the pace to slip, it should be quite fast-moving.・

CHARACTERS: NARRATOR – female, pleasant and bouncy, in charge, holds the whole thing together; she is firm but kind with:

A&B – mischievous lads who tease the NARRATOR. Their sole aim is to have good fun.

NASTY ZAC – wears cloth cap, long mac and has a bag or large pouch. He is thoroughly mean and twisted. (Although not so much as to cause smaller children to burst into tears.)

A row of four brightly coloured chairs set USC. NARRATOR
DSC *gives a largely improvised introduction suited to the
situation, mentioning that they are going to act a story from
the Bible, and how they looked through the Bible to find one,
etc., and such things as 'we want to tell you a story about how
Jesus can change people' and 'not just changing people
on the outside but deep inside', etc., during this* A&B *are
naughtily upstaging her by creeping surreptitiously towards
each other from opposite sides of the stage.* NARRATOR
catches them at it a couple of times. A&B *play innocent.*
NARRATOR *attempts to carry on as normal, but with difficulty. Eventually* A&B *meet* CS *and by intertwining with
arms outstretched make a tree shape immediately behind*
NARRATOR CS *but* DS *of chairs.*

NARRATOR: (*giving up introduction, moves to one
side*) What are you doing?

A&B: (*proudly*) We're a tree!

NARRATOR: (*to audience*) They're a tree! Just
ignore them – perhaps they'll go
away. (*Resumes* DSC *position.*) Right
(*recapping*) so we tried to think
of a story about how Jesus can
change . . . (A&B *interrupt with a loud
screeching, creaking noise as they
sway in one direction*).

NARRATOR: (*trying to ignore it and carry on*) . . .
but however hard we tried, we . . .
(*They screech again, swaying the
opposite way.* NARRATOR *is ruffled.*)
. . . so we thought and thought . . .
and . . . (*Screech again.* NARRATOR
gives up. Moves to side again.)
What's that supposed to be?

A: Tree noises!

NARRATOR: Trees don't make noises.

B: They do when they've got the
wind . . .

A: . . . blowing through their branches.

NARRATOR: (*resigned*) Right. Tree noises. Fine
. . . (*resumes position and attempts to
continue. The creaking and swaying
become so frantic she has to give up
despite her attempts to shout over the
noise.* A&B *giggle naughtily.*) Look!
How can I talk to all these people
and tell them our story when you
keep making noises and making them
laugh?

A: (*breaking pose slightly*) Yes, but
what *we* say is . . . can't we do a story
with a tree in it?

B: Yeah. And we'll be the tree.

A: Yeah! (*They resume tree.*)

NARRATOR: (*thinking*) A story with a tree in it
. . . we didn't plan to do . . . (*She has
an idea.*) Oh, yes! I've thought of a
story with a tree in it!

A&B: Great! (*They inject extra enthusiasm
to tree shape.*)

NARRATOR: But the tree doesn't come into it
right at the beginning . . .

A&B: (*disappointed*) Oh.

NARRATOR: Not until at least half-way through.

A&B: (*deflated. They look at each other
nose to nose.*) Oh.

NARRATOR: So if you'd like to wait over there
(*indicating* SL), I'll let you know
when we need the tree.

B: (*moving* SL) You promise?

NARRATOR: I promise.

A: (*moving* SL) You won't forget to tell
us?

NARRATOR: I won't forget. (A&B *stand poised.*)
Right. We're going to tell you a story
with a tree in it, and . . . (A&B *noisily
rush* CS *and take up their tree*

| | *position*.) Not yet! (*There is a brief pause,* NARRATOR *is exasperated*.) Did I say I wanted the tree? |

A&B: We thought you did.

NARRATOR: Just wait over there, and I'll tell you when it's your turn.

B: (*moving* SL *again*) You promise?

NARRATOR: I promise.

A: (*moving* SL) You won't forget?

NARRATOR: I won't forget. Actually, before you're the tree, I want you to be the people.

A&B: What people?

NARRATOR: The people of the town.

A&B: What town?

NARRATOR: The town of Jericho.

A: (*moving* CS) Jerry who?

B: (*moving to* A) Hey, isn't he the brother of Doctor Who?

A: Jerry Who! (*They both fall about laughing*.)

B: Every one a gem. Boom boom!

NARRATOR: (*interrupting*) The town of Jericho.

A&B: (*realising they are being silly*) Oh!

NARRATOR: And they were very tall people, very big people . . . so if you'd like to stand up here (*indicating the chairs* US).

A: (*climbing on to them*) Tall people?

NARRATOR: Tall people.

B: (*climbing up also*) Big people?

NARRATOR: Big people. (A *takes up a tall, strong-man pose.* B *tries to copy but ends up with a grotesque caricature.* A *falls about laughing again,* NARRATOR *stopping them*.) Just people. (A&B *stand still and watch*.) Right! We're going to tell you a story, and it's all

about a man called Nasty Zac, and
. . . (*loud disturbance at the back of
the auditorium as* NASTY ZAC *enters
behind the audience with a loud
cough.*)

ZAC: I hate Christians! I hate Manchester!
I hate kids! (*or appropriate regional
and situational alternatives. He stands*
DSL *glaring at children with an
ultra-nasty expression.*) Nyi! (*to* A&B)
Nyi! (*he turns back to the audience
gloating.* A&B *poke tongues out, pull
faces, etc., behind his back. He
suddenly turns to face them.* A&B *jump
to neutral positions.*) Nyi!

NARRATOR: (*whispering*) This is Nasty Zac.
This is the story of Nasty Zac.
A mean old man who wears a mac.
Although he wasn't very big.
(*Indicating* A&B.) They hated him
and called him . . .

A&B: (*to* ZAC *with venom*)   . . . Pig!

NARRATOR: He went and knocked on every door
Demanding money from rich and
poor.
And even if you couldn't pay
Still he wouldn't go away.
He'd kill your cat and smash your
telly,
Until he'd got your very last penny!
(NARRATOR *joins* A&B *on the chairs*
SR. NASTY ZAC *moves* SL *off the chairs
and 'knocks' on an imaginary
door.*)

ZAC: Knock, knock, knock!

A: Watch out! Watch out!

B: He's coming back.

NARRATOR: Who can it be?

A&B & NAR: (*they are all terrified.*) It's Nasty Zac!

ZAC: (*impatient*) Knock, knock, knock!

NARRATOR: We'd better let him in.

A: (*indicating* B) Y . . . y . . . y . . . *you* open the door.

B: Me? (*Swallowing audibly. He mimes opening a door.*)

ZAC: (*jumps in and points at* A) You owe me money!

A: I don't!

ZAC: (*moving along and pointing at* B) *You* owe me money!

B: I don't!

ZAC: (*moves and points at* NARRATOR) And you owe me money!

NARRATOR: I don't!

ZAC: In fact all three of you owe me money.

A&B & NAR: We don't.

ZAC: Yes you do.

A&B & NAR: Oh no we don't!

ZAC: Oh yes you do!

A&B & NAR: Oh no we don't!

ZAC: (*angrily*) Cut the theatricals!
If you won't give me any money,
I'll kill your cat and smash your telly,
Until I get your very last penny!
(*Holding out hand to* NARRATOR.) So pay up!

NARRATOR: But we really haven't got any money. (*Makes suitable spent-up gesture.*)

B: Nothing at all. (*Copies gesture.*)

A: Not even a penny. (*Copies again.*)

B: Farthing.

ZAC: Absolutely nothing?

A&B & NAR: (*using the gesture to stress*)
Absolutely nothing!

ZAC: Right you rotten lot, if you haven't got any money, then I'll have to have something else instead. (*Paces around the front of the stage.*) Now what can I have? What can I take off you? Ah, I know (*with a sadistic gleam*), if you haven't got any money, then I'll just have to have . . . your Smarties!

A&B & NAR: Smarties?

ZAC: Yes, your Smarties.

A&B & NAR: (*melodramatic, with suitable poses*) Not our Smarties!

ZAC: Yes, your Smarties. Come on pay up. (*He goes along the line taking Smarties from each of them in turn. They are all crying and fumbling in their pockets. He holds out his bag for them to drop their Smarties in.*)

NARRATOR: Ooh! (*Drops them in.*)

ZAC: Come on, come on!

B: I was saving all the orange ones. (*Drops orange ones in.*)

ZAC: I love orange ones!

A: It's my last few . . . (*Drops some in.*)

ZAC: Good. (*Turns away from them.*) Mmm, I love Smarties . . . (A *has kept one Smartie and is being encouraged by the others to eat it.* ZAC *notices and leaps, catching* A's *wrist.*) In the bag!

A: But it's my last one and I . . .

ZAC: In the bag! (A *drops it in reluctantly.*) Mmm. (ZAC *greedily stuffs Smarties in his mouth.* DSL *he glares at the audience and exits* SL.)

A&B & NAR: Boo! Boo! Ssss! (*encouraging audience to join in.*)

NARRATOR: (*jumping off chair* DSR) The boos of the crowd soon turned to . . .

A&B & NAR: Hooray!

NARRATOR: For something special was happening that day
For in that town there soon would be
Someone everyone wanted to see.

B: Hey Janet! (*Or relevant name.*) Look over here! *He beckons vigorously.* NARRATOR *joins them on the chairs again. All three turn facing* US. *They mime clapping, chanting, etc., as if a football crowd. enter* ZAC.)

ZAC: What's going on? (*To audience.*) Who is this person everyone wants to see? Who is it? (*Taunting them.*) Won't anybody tell me? (*They shout* 'no!') Don't you like me or something? (*They shout again.*) Right, you rotten lot! If you won't tell me who this special person is, I'll just have to see for myself. (*He tries to see through, past, over, etc., the three on chairs, but is unable to do so.*) It's no good. I can't see, I'm not tall enough. Ah! I know. I'll climb up a tree; that way I'll be able to see who this special person is. (*He looks about the stage for a tree.*) There's supposed to be a tree here somewhere! (*He taps the* NARRATOR.) Oi you!

NARRATOR: Yes?

ZAC: Where's the tree?

NARRATOR: What tree?

ZAC: The tree that's supposed to be here for me to climb up to see who the special person is, you fool!

NARRATOR: Don't call me a fool. I'm not the one who wanted to be a tree, (*to audience*) am I? (*indicating* A&B *who are still waving, etc.*) It's them. (*She taps* B. *They stop waving and turn.*) It's now! (A&B *look confused.*) The bit with the tree . . . (A&B *still more confused. She appeals to the audience.*) Go on. Tell them! (A&B *realise.*)

A&B: (*excited*) The tree! (*They jump down and form their 'tree', immediately* DS *of the chairs.*)

ZAC: Ah! Now I can climb up a tree and see who the special person is. (A&B *look shocked and worried.*)

B: Wait a minute! Nobody said anything about climbing.

A: No.

ZAC: Shut up! (*To audience.*) I've heard of whispering grass but this is ridiculous. (*He starts to climb. They start to object.*) Be quiet! Trees don't talk! (*He climbs the 'tree'. Their creaking noise resumes as* ZAC *climbs, but turns into cries of pain. He perches on their shoulders. To audience.*) Ah, it's Jesus!

NARRATOR: (*jumping off chair*, DSR)
Just as Jesus was passing by
Something in the tree-top caught his eye.
The crowd were really taken aback,
When Jesus went over and talked to Zac!
Then, said Zac, from the top of his tree:

ZAC: Good Lord! He wants to come round for tea! (*He begins to climb down the tree; he clouts* A's *head on the way.*) Stupid tree! *Beckoning to an imaginary Jesus.*) Come on, it's this way. Come along Jesus. We can have Smarties for tea. (*Exit* SL. A&B *resume their swaying and creaking. It has developed into a silly tune, e.g. the Laurel and Hardy theme.*)

NARRATOR: (*not wanting to appear unkind*) Er . . . that's it . . . (A&B *continue.*) The end . . . (A&B *stop. A last creak turns into a question*):

B: Eeurk?

NARRATOR: That's the end of the bit with the tree . . . sorry.

A: Already?

B: Oh, I was just getting into that . . .

A: Yeah.

NARRATOR: Yes, I'm sorry. (*A new idea.*) Actually, I'd like you to be the people again.

A&B: Right!

B: (*moves* DSL *to audience*) Fancy Jesus talking to someone as horrible as Nasty Zac!

NARRATOR: (*moves* DS *next to* B *to audience*) Yeah, and he's even gone to his house. I don't know how he could do it.

A: (*moves* DS *next to* NARRATOR. *To audience*) Especially when Nasty Zac has got all my Smarties!

B&NAR: Yeah!

B: Hey! (*Jumping on to chairs and looking* DSL *with eyes shaded.*) Let's see what they're doing!

NARRATOR: (*standing in front of chairs, looking* DSL *with eyes shaded*) Let's see what they're saying!

A: (*crouches in front of* NARRATOR *looking* DSL *with eyes shaded*) Let's see what they're eating! (*During this section the pitch gets higher and higher.*)

B: (*to audience, then resuming 'looking' pose*) They're talking to each other.

NARRATOR: (*to audience, then resuming 'looking' pose*) Jesus is telling Zac he's nasty.

A: (*to audience, then resuming 'looking' pose*) They're eating strawberry jam.

B: (*as before*) Zac's saying he's sorry.

NARRATOR: (*as before*) They're shaking hands!

A: (*as before*) They're eating cream doughnuts!

B: (*as before*) Now he's getting his purse out!

NARRATOR: (*as before*) He says he's going to give all that money back.

A: (*to* NARRATOR) Hey! Hey! Does that mean I'll get my Smarties back?

B: (*top falsetto*) Oh, I should think so, Robin. (*Relevant name. He realises the pitch is ridiculous and drops to deep bass.*) I should think so Robin.

A: Oh, great!

NARRATOR: (*moves away from looking*) Hey you two, it's not right looking through people's windows to see what they're doing.

B: (*looking at* NARRATOR) No, but it's good fun though innit? (*Looks back* OSL.)

NARRATOR: (*with discipline in her voice*) Stephen! (*Relevant name.* B *shrugs and stops*

'looking'. A *joins him on the chairs.*
NARRATOR *comes* DSR.)
Jesus talked to Zac all night
And Zac admitted he'd not been
right.
Instead of being

B:	nasty
NARRATOR:	and
A:	mean.

NARRATOR: He'd changed to the
A&B & NAR: nicest person
you've ever seen.

NARRATOR: And Zac is still nice to this very day
Instead of taking, he gives away!
(*She joins* A&B *on chairs.*)

ZAC: (*from* os) Whoopee! (*He enters and
runs* DSC, *having excitedly waved to
the audience.*)
Although I've been bad for many
days,
I want to change my wicked ways.
Jesus told me why I'm sad,
I'll never be happy so long as I'm
bad.
So as sure as my name is Mister
Zac . . .
I'm going to give all their money
back!

NARRATOR: Great!

B: Super!

A: Fantastic!

NARRATOR: And for all the people I've hurt,
I'll throw great big parties.
I'll even give them back (*indicating
A&B & NARRATOR*) their Smarties!

A&B & NAR: (*obviously delighted*) Smarties!

ZAC: Come on hold out your hands!
(*Going along the line dishing out*

	handfuls of Smarties. To NARRATOR) Some for you. (*To* B.) Tons·for you. (*To* A.) And mega-tons for Robin.
NARRATOR:	There's twice as many as I had before!
B:	Three times as many!
A:	Four times as many! (*They all jump off their chairs and come* DSL *around* ZAC.)
A&B & NAR:	Thank you Mr Zac!
ZAC:	And those I've left, I know what I'll do. I'll not eat them myself, I'll give them to you! (*Indicates audience.*)
A&B & NAR:	(*ad lib.*) Yeah! Great! (*All four actors rush into audience distributing Smarties liberally.*)

BE A HERO

This is basically a dramatised story for children but we have found that its knock-about humour appeals to all ages when they are in a relaxed situation. It is a parallel version of 'The Good Samaritan'. It couldn't really be called a modern version as it is set in the Middle Ages. The script demands audience participation at a very basic level, but there is room for you to add your own topical comments or local references as the general atmosphere of the piece is that of a group of actors 'playing' at being in the story, and should give a feeling of shared good fun.

CHARACTERS: MELVYN – a medieval minstrel dressed in a bright costume, a little like the Joker from a pack of cards. He wears tights and (if possible) carries a guitar with which he accompanies the musical parts of the sketch. If it is not possible for the actor to play an instrument the accompaniment may be provided by a separate musician sitting to one side of the action. Melvyn is cheerful and a little cheeky.

PRINCESS JOANNE – a spoilt little girl pretending to be a beautiful princess. She wears a tall steeple hat or tiny crown and speaks with a lisp.

BIFF and SWIPE – a couple of Dennis-the-Menace ruffians. They are dressed scruffily and are constantly arguing and fighting together.

Despite this they are the best of
friends and are actually quite lovable.

PROPS: Guitar (or other musical instrument)
A prince's hat with a feather
A pair of horse's 'reins'
Coconut shells – for horse's hooves
A knight's helmet
A toy sword
A pig mask
A smelly, dirty costume of rags
A row of colourful chairs, a low table
or a stage block at the back of the
acting area on which the props are
ranged

MELVYN: (*Enters whistling to himself, notices
the audience, looks surprised at their
presence then addresses them with a
loud greeting.*)
Hello everybody!
(*The audience presumably respond.*)
That was pathetic! I'm sure you can
do better than that, (etc) . . .
(*Tries again, this time shouting
enthusiastically.*)
Hello everybody!
(*The audience should respond more
readily.*)
Hello, my name is Melvyn and I'm a
minstrel. That's supposed to explain
the tights! In olden days minstrels like
me used to go round singing songs
and telling stories, and that's just
what I'm going to do. I'm going to
sing you a song and tell you a story all
about what it's like to be a real hero.

JOANNE: (*running in and interrupting him*)

Ooh! Can I be in your story please?

MELVYN: (*looking amazed*) Who are you?

JOANNE: I'm a princess, and princesses are always looking for handsome heroes to fall in love with.

MELVYN: This isn't a fairy story you know, it's from the Bible.

JOANNE: But it has got a hero in it?

MELVYN: Yes.

JOANNE: Right (*stamping her foot and pouting*). I want to be in it then.

MELVYN: All right, what's your name?

JOANNE: Joanne, Princess Joanne.

MELVYN: A real princess, eh? There's one thing about this story, it's got a song in it, and the song's got clapping.

JOANNE: Clapping?

MELVYN: Yes, so when I stamp my foot twice, like this (*he demonstrates*) you have to clap your hands twice, like this. (*He claps twice.*) OK?

JOANNE: Well (*doubtfully*), I'll try.
(*They practise one chorus of the song.* JOANNE *isn't very good.*)

MELVYN: That was useless! I bet these people here (*indicating audience*) can do better than that. Come on, let's have a go; when I stamp my foot, you clap twice. Show Princess Joanne how intelligent you are here in Nottingham.
(*Substitute the name of local area, etc. They practise chorus again, this time with the audience's help.* JOANNE *is much better.*)
Brilliant! Right then, a story about Princess Joanne and a real hero. Let the story commence.

(*Sings.*)
I'll tell you a story, so pin back your lug-holes.
Of a time long ago, in a faraway land.
There lived a fair maiden, dressed up for a journey,
Her name was the beautiful Princess Joanne.

BOTH: (*sing*) Princess Joanne, Princess Joanne (*with clapping*).

JOANNE: (*sings*) My name is the beautiful Princess Joanne.
(*As the refrain finishes* BIFF *and* SWIPE *enter noisily – if possible through the audience or from* SR.)

SWIPE: Look it's Melvyn.

BOTH: 'Ello Melvyn. (*To audience.*) 'Ello.

MELVYN: Oh no! I thought that for once I could tell a story without you great oafs coming along.

SWIPE: Where's your manners then? Introduce us.

MELVYN: Ladies and gentlemen, Biff and Swipe.

BIFF: I'm Biff.

SWIPE: And I'm Swipe.

BIFF: (*biffing* SWIPE *in the stomach*) Biff!

SWIPE: (*swiping* BIFF *round the head*) Swipe!
(*They laugh, shake hands and address audience in unison.*)

BOTH: We like fighting.

BIFF: Can we be in your story, Melvyn?

MELVYN: Yes, I suppose so.

SWIPE: Has it got a fight in it?

MELVYN: Yes it has.

BOTH: (*jumping and shadow boxing*) Oh great . . . Who do we fight? Who do we fight? (MELVYN *points at* JOANNE. *They stop.*) Her?

MELVYN: Yes, her. Now look, Princess Joanne
is going on a walk through the dark
forest, so hide behind some trees.
Quick.
(*They pretend to hide.*)
Let the story begin.

JOANNE: I'm off in search of a handsome hero.
(*Sings.*) 'Some day my Prince will
come'.
(*They jump out at her.*)

SWIPE: (*shouts*) Ambush!

JOANNE: (*screams*) Ah!
(*She assumes exaggerated pose of
shock and horror.*)

BIFF: Your money or your life!

JOANNE: You can have my money.
(*Hands them her purse.*)

SWIPE: We'll have her life anyway.
(*They beat her up in a short comical
slapstick fight during which they shout
'swipe' and 'biff' with every blow. She
faints melodramatically and they
return to* USC *to await next instruction
from* MELVYN.)

MELVYN: (*sings*) The Princess was lying in a
heap by the roadside,
When along came Prince Ivor whose
looks were so good . . .

BIFF & SWIPE: (*interrupting with hands up as at
school*) Melvyn?

MELVYN: What?

BOTH: (*in unison*) I want to be Prince Ivor.

BIFF: Is he the hero?

SWIPE: Of course he's the hero!

BOTH: (*arguing and almost coming to blows*)
I want to be the hero, etc.

MELVYN: (*tries to quieten them down and
eventually shouts to drown them out*)

Shut up! Let me finish the verse.

BOTH: (*in unison*) Sorry Melvyn.

MELVYN: (*sings*) He rode in his carriage so gleaming and spotless,
When he spied the fair maiden in a great pool of blood.

ALL: (*sing*) Great pool of blood, great pool of blood (*with clapping*).
He spied the fair maiden, in a great pool of blood.
(JOANNE *groans and moans from her position on the ground as* BIFF *and* SWIPE *fight over the prince's hat. They snatch it from each other until eventually* SWIPE *puts it on*)

SWIPE: (*proudly*) Prince Ivor.

BIFF: (*snatches it off him while he's not looking and puts it on.*)
I'm Prince Ivor. You can be my horse and carriage.
(*He puts reins around* SWIPE*'s neck.*)
Gee up Neddy!
(*They trot around the stage; as they pass the Princess she calls out to them.*)

JOANNE: (*weakly*) Help! Help! Help!

BIFF: Whoa!
(BIFF *stops and hauls* SWIPE *back so that they crash into each other.* BIFF *picks himself up and indicates* JOANNE.)
A princess in distress. I must go and help her.

JOANNE: (*to audience*) A handsome prince in a carriage to carry me off and rescue me. My hero!

BIFF: (*proudly*) Oh yes!

MELVYN: Oh no!

BIFF: Eh?

MELVYN: Prince Ivor isn't the hero.

BIFF: (*disappointed*) Oh . . . (*to Princess*) I am sorry, fair princess, but I cannot rescue you today. I've just had my carriage seats recovered and you might get blood all over them. Gee up, Neddy.
(*They trot back to position* USC *and replace props.*)

MELVYN: (*sings*) The Prince drove his carriage off into the sunset,
When along came a knight on a stallion white.

BOTH: (*interrupting as before*) Melvyn?

MELVYN: What?

BOTH: I want to be the knight on a stallion white.

BIFF: Is he the hero?

SWIPE: Of course he's the hero!

BOTH: (*fighting as before*) I want to be the hero, etc.

MELVYN: Sh-h-h-h-h-h!

BIFF: Have you got a gas leak, Melvyn?

MELVYN: No I have not. Let me finish the verse.

BOTH: Sorry Melvyn!

MELVYN: (*sings*) With sharp sword in hand, how he looked very charming,
He came to the Princess and noticed her plight.

ALL: Noticed her plight, noticed her plight (*with clapping*).
He came to the Princess and noticed her plight.
(JOANNE *groans as before.* SWIPE, *wearing a knight's helmet, jumps piggy-back style on to* BIFF's *back and holds up a toy sword. They trot*

around the stage. BIFF *holds coconut
shells with which he makes
horse's-hoof sounds.*)

JOANNE: Help! Help! Help!

SWIPE: Whoa!
(*They stop moving, but horse's hoof
noise continues.*)
Shut-up!
(*They stop.*)

JOANNE: (*indicating* SWIPE *to audience*) Ah! A
knight on a stallion white. He's come
to rescue me. My hero!

SWIPE: Never fear, damson in distress, for I
will get off my horse and rescue you.
(*He jumps down, but bounces back
almost immediately as* MELVYN
interrupts.)

MELVYN: No you won't!

SWIPE: No I won't! Why not?

MELVYN: Because the knight on the stallion
white isn't the hero either.

SWIPE: (*puzzled*) Oh . . . I cannot stop and
help you now fair maiden for I am a
bad knight and not a good knight.

BIFF: So good night.

SWIPE: Sleep tight.

BOTH: Mind the bugs don't bite!
(*They gallop back to position* USC
*with more coconut effects and return
the props. During the next verse the
princess makes a valiant attempt to get
to her feet but fails pathetically.*)

MELVYN: (*sings*) Princess Joanne, she had just
about had it.
(*She groans.*)
When along came a stranger they
called 'Will the Swill'. . . .
(*anticipating their interruption*)

What?

BOTH: (*interrupting once more but realising that* MELVYN *has beaten them to it. Looking at each other*) Eh? (*Recovering.*) I want to be Will the Swill.

MELVYN: But you don't know anything about Will the Swill. For instance – he works with pigs.

BOTH: Uurgh!

MELVYN: He's very smelly.

BOTH: (*holding noses*) Pooh!

MELVYN: He's got horrible warts and sores all over his body.

BOTH: (*pushing each other away*) Uurgh!

MELVYN: And his best friend is a pig. (*Goes to sing.*)

BOTH: Melvyn!

MELVYN: What?

BOTH: I want to be the pig!

SWIPE: Is the pig the hero?

MELVYN: No, he's not. (*Sings.*)
With his best friend the pig, he'd just come from the pig farm,
With his warts and his smell he did make you feel ill, etc.

ALL: Make you feel ill, make you feel ill (*with clapping*).
With his warts and his smell he did make you feel ill.
(MELVYN *kicks 'Will the Swill' costume to* BIFF *and* SWIPE. *They fight to avoid holding it.*)

BIFF & SWIPE: You can be him
Phew this stinks
I don't want to be him, etc.

MELVYN: Get on with it.
(BIFF *puts on costume, while* SWIPE

puts on pig mask.)

SWIPE: Oink! Oink!

BIFF: It's not fair! Why do I get the smelly parts?
(SWIPE *makes 'you smell' signs.* BIFF *kicks him.*)
Shaddup you! Come on piggy (*pushing him*) off to market with you . . .

SWIPE: Don't touch me, you smell!

BIFF: I can't help it! Go on!
(*They walk round Joanne* DS.)

JOANNE: Help!

SWIPE: Oink.

JOANNE: (*weakly*) Help!

SWIPE: Oink.

BIFF: Wait! What's that?

SWIPE: (*putting mask up*) It was an oink.

JOANNE: (*very weakly*) Help!

BIFF: No . . . that. A princess in distress, but I can't help her; she's a princess and I'm just a pig boy!
(*He starts to exit sadly.*)

MELVYN: Yes you can, go and help her.

BIFF: But she's all royal, and I'm all pongy.

MELVYN: But that doesn't matter; I'm telling this story, and I say you can go and help her. So go on, off you go.

BIFF: Oh thank you, Melvyn.
(JOANNE *groans.*)
My princess!

JOANNE: My hero?

BIFF: Come, I will bandage up your wounds. Look at these sores. But don't worry, (*to audience*) I'll take her back to my pig farm and rub some oinkment on them. (*To* JOANNE.)
Come, I will put you on my pig. (*To*

SWIPE.) Oi, pig face! Over here!
(*She jumps on* SWIPE's *back.*) That
must be where they get piggy-back
from!

MELVYN: And so, Will the Swill took the
princess back to his house, where she
stayed until she was completely
better. The end.
(*He starts to bow.*)

BIFF: Melvyn!

MELVYN: What?

BIFF: But who was the hero?

MELVYN: Well who do you think acted like a
hero?

BIFF: Eh?

MELVYN: Who helped the princess?

BIFF: (*realising*) Will the Swill (*indicating
himself*).

MELVYN: Right, so Will the Swill is the hero.
You see . . . (*Sings.*)
You don't have to be rich, you don't
have to be clever,
The same thing is true for all people
you know.
As God has loved us, we must love
one another.
Love everybody, you'll be a hero,
etc.

ALL: Be a hero, be a hero (*with clapping*)
Love everybody, you'll be a hero.

MELVYN: (*Repeats as others take up a suitable
tableau.*)
As God has loved us, we must love
one another.
Love everybody, you'll be a hero.

ALL: Be a hero, be a hero (*with clapping*)
Love everybody, you'll be a hero.
(*All bow.*)

BE A HERO

1. I'll tell you a story so pin back your lug'oles.
   Of a time long ago in a faraway land
   There lived a fair maiden dressed up for a journey,
   Her name was the beautiful Princess Joanne.
   Princess Joanne. Princess Joanne.
   Her name was the beautiful Princess Joanne.

2. The Princess was lying in a heap by the roadside,
   When along came Prince Ivor whose looks were so
      good.
   He rode in his carriage all gleaming and spotless
   When he spied the fair maiden in a great pool of blood.
   Great pool of blood, great pool of blood.
   He spied the fair maiden in a great pool of blood.

3. The Prince drove his carriage off into the sunset
   When along came a Knight on a stallion white.
   With sharp sword in hand how he looked very
      charming,
   He came to the Princess and noticed her plight.
   Noticed her plight. Noticed her plight.
   He came to the Princess and noticed her plight.

4. Princess Joanne she had just about had it.
   When along came a stranger they called Will the Swill,
   With his best friend the pig they'd just come from the
      pig-farm.
   With his warts and his smell they did make you feel ill.
   Make you feel ill. Make you feel ill.
   With his warts and his smell they did make you feel ill.

5. You don't have to be rich, you don't have to be clever.
   The same thing is true for all people you know:
   As God has loved us we must love one another.
   Love everybody, you'll be a hero.
   Be a hero. Be a hero.
   Love everybody, you'll be a hero.

Trad.

I'll tell you a sto-ry so pin back your lug-holes. In a

time long a - go in a   far a - way land, there

lived a fair mai-den dressed up for a   jour-ney. Her

name was the beau-ti - ful Prin-cess Jo - anne,

Prin - cess Jo - anne,   Prin - cess Jo - anne. Her

name was the beau-ti - ful Prin-cess Jo - anne.

RSVP

Hardly a drama, more of an introduction to the topic of God's Kingdom, or the acceptance of every type of person. Particularly suitable for younger children.

CHARACTERS: PERCY POSH – impeccably dressed, well groomed. Upper class, very well spoken.

SIDNEY SCRUFF – a rough, muddied mess. Very badly spoken. Wears tattered short trousers.

PERCY *and* SID *enter simultaneously brandishing identical letters.*

BOTH: I've got a letter! I've got a letter!
(*Noticing the other. With disdain.*)
Oh, it's you.

PERCY: (*to audience*) Fancy bumping into Sidney Scruff on such a lovely Sunday morning.

SID: (*to audience*) Fancy bumping into Percy Posh on a Sunday morning.

PERCY: (*taunting* SID) My dad's better than your dad.

SID: (*not to be outdone*) My dad's better than your dad.

PERCY: No he isn't!

SID: Yes he is!

PERCY: Isn't!

SID: Is!

PERCY: (*importantly to audience*) My dad's on the town council.

SID: (*to audience*) My dad's on the dole.

PERCY: My dad's got a Rolls Royce.

SID: My dad's got a rusty old bike.

PERCY: My dad's had tea with the Queen.

SID: My dad's . . . (*having trouble*) . . . my dad's . . .

PERCY: Yes?

SID: My dad . . . (*victorious!*) goes down the pub with the Queen!

PERCY: No he doesn't!

SID: Yes he does!

PERCY: Doesn't!

SID: Does!

PERCY: Doesn't!

SID: Does! (*This accelerates and degenerates into a verbal squabble, culminating with poking out of tongues. They turn away from each other in a huff.*)

PERCY: I'm going to open my letter. I wonder who it's from? It's a very posh envelope.

SID: I'm going to open my letter. I hope it's from Man. United asking me to play centre forward. (*They both open them.*)

BOTH: It's from the King! (*They look at each other.*)

PERCY: Let me have a look at that.

SID: Let me have a look at that.

BOTH: (*looking at each other's letter*) His Majesty the King, requests the pleasure of (*they look disdainfully at each other*) *your* company at a Royal Party.

PERCY: (*to audience*) How spiffing! A party!

I'll wear my new superduper suit!

SID: (*to audience*) A party! Nifty! I might even wash my knees.

PERCY: (*self-importantly*) I bet you it's not the same party as mine.

SID: Bet you it is.

PERCY: Isn't.

SID: Is.

PERCY: When's yours?

SID: (*reads*) Saturday.

PERCY: (*reads his. Worried*) So is mine. Ah! But what time?

SID: (*reads*) Two thirty.

PERCY: (*reads. Horrified*) So is mine! (SID *laughs silently, pointing to* PERCY. *They put their letters away.* PERCY *realises he must relent, albeit unwillingly.*) Sidney?

SID: What is it Perce?

PERCY: I was thinking . . .

SID: Yeah?

PERCY: (*awkwardly*) Well, seeing as how we're going to the same party . . . well, why don't we go together?

SID: (*conceding*) Oh . . . all right.

PERCY: Daddy can give us a lift in his Rolls Royce.

SID: (*lights up*) Oh . . . great!

PERCY: Come on then. (*They link arms as though the greatest of friends. They make to go. Pause.*)

BOTH: (*to audience. Aside, pointing to the other*) They'll think he's in fancy dress! (*Both laugh, Exeunt.*)

SIGNS AND BLUNDERS

This is a participatory drama in three sections. The idea is not only to engage the congregation's attention but also to provide an opportunity for physical involvement, albeit limited, to encourage a tangible response to the message. Everyone present should not be regarded as audience but rather as worshippers (including the actors) rediscovering the story together. Close liaison with the minister or person leading the worship is vital in order to key into other parts of the service, e.g. prayers, songs, etc. It is a good idea if all three sections follow quite closely on each other (the momentum gained in the first episode is easily lost by the time the third one starts). GOD may be situated in the pulpit, JONAH on the opposite side. CARDHOLDERS should be situated where the cards may be easily seen but not so as to intrude on what's going on between GOD and JONAH. Time, effort and a little money need to be spent on the cards; lettering should be big, bold and colourful.

CHARACTERS: GOD – A cheerful young woman with a lot of presence!

JONAH – A coward. A moaner. If he wears thick glasses so much the better.

CARDHOLDERS – Two alert people with strong arms! (They need have no acting skills.)

Note: All characters make the appropriate responses to the cards along with the congregation; except JONAH in obvious instances.

ONE

GOD: Good morning, St Nic's (*name of church*). You may not recognise me straight off but I'm God. I'm sure you'll get used to me as time goes on. Now then, I'd like you to meet a servant of mine. Jonah . . . Jonah?

JONAH: (*hunched over a large scroll, writing with a quill*) Somebody call? Did somebody say my name? (*To congregation.*) Who called me? (*They hopefully give the answer.*) God? . . . Oh not again, er . . . I mean . . . how wonderful!

GOD: Hello Jonah. How are your memoirs coming along? He's writing a book all about his life. Have you finished it?

JONAH: Er . . . nearly.

GOD: Where are you up to?

JONAH: The title.

GOD: I might have guessed. Read it out.

JONAH: (*clears his throat, etc.*) 'Jonah – he got it right.'

GOD: Wrong.

JONAH: Is it? Oh dear – is it my spelling?

GOD: It should be 'Jonah – he got it wrong'; right?

JONAH: But I *did* get it right.

GOD: In the end. (*To congregation.*) Look, we'll all have to help him with his memoirs. Will you help me? (*Response.*) Good. Right, first of all tell him what he did when I told him to go and preach at Nineveh. Who can tell him? (*Response, ad lib.*) Remember, Jonah?

JONAH: (*sheepish*) Yeah, come to think of it I do now . . . (*He writes.*)

GOD: Alleluia! Lesson number one: Jonah learns the hard way how to say 'yes' to God. Got that?

JONAH: Er . . . how do you spell Alleluia?

GOD: (*sighs*) You'll have to help him with this. Every time they (*indicates cardholders*) hold up a sign, you shout it out. Like this. (CARDHOLDERS *hold up a card with the words* 'Go to Nineveh' *on it. Ad lib. In order to get it right, etc.*) I said to him, 'That city needs my help.' But Jonah said,

JONAH: No thanks, I fancy Spain myself. Benidorm's rather nice this time of year. (CARD: '*Olé!*')

GOD: You've got to be quick with these (*repeat if necessary*).
You see I had a special job for Jonah but he said (CARD: 'No').
So I had to think quick. Jonah had caught a boat so I arranged a big storm out at sea. Meanwhile Jonah was sleeping in the hold. (CARD: 'Zzzzzzz'.)

JONAH: (*snoring*) Viva España!

GOD: Then the boat hit a storm. Right this is where it gets exciting – all of you over there, I want you to go: (CARDHOLDER 1 *on appropriate side joins in.*) 'Rumble rumble'. (Followed by two claps in the same rhythm; she rehearses the congregation in this.) These people here, you're the wind. (CARDHOLDERS 1 & 2 *both join in.*) 'Whoosh! Howl! Moan!' (*They practise.*) And you can all be the waves: 'Splish!

Splash! Splosh!' (*They practise.*)
All together now. (*They do.*) Still Jonah
slept on (CARD: 'Zzzzzzz') and the
storm got louder (*She devises an action
for control of volume.*) All the
sailors were worried (CARD: 'We're
worried'). And they consulted
their gods and idols for help.

CARDHOLDER 1: (*reading imaginary magazine*) Pisces:
Enjoy yourself and relax. Today is
your day for travel and excitement.
Tut!

GOD: I keep telling them to stop reading
them, but they never take any notice.
Anyway, the sailors discovered that
it was all Jonah's fault.

JONAH: (*melodramatically*) It is God himself
who has brought this storm! The
Lord of Heaven and Earth! I am
running away from him and now he is
punishing me for being so stupid.
Throw me over the side! I might as
well die!

GOD: And the storm raged on. (*She signals
again. Congregation respond with
storm noises.*) The sailors got more
worried!

JONAH: Go on throw me in! It's all my fault!

GOD: So they did. (*Storm noise increases
then stops.*)

JONAH: Ah ha! (CARD: 'Kersplosh!').

GOD: And the storm died down and
everything was quiet. The sailors
were happy; but Jonah wasn't. You
see I had a special job for Jonah but
he said (CARD: 'No'). Do you
remember now Jonah?

JONAH: Yes, I thought I was a goner.

GOD: Did I give up on you?

JONAH: No.

GOD: Did I leave you to die?

JONAH: No.

GOD: What did I do?

JONAH: You showed me how much you love me.

GOD: Well done! I showed Jonah how much I loved him by sending a great big fish to swallow him up! You might be thinking, 'What a funny way to show someone that you love them.' Well, just think, it could have been a shark!

JONAH: (*begrudgingly*) Yes – thank you Lord for allowing me to be swallowed by that great big fish – (*sarcastically*) that was really fantastic!

GOD: Don't laugh. He means it. He could have been drowned. You see I had a special job for Jonah but he said (CARD: 'No'). I did all this to protect him and help him to understand that he should have said (CARD: 'Yes, Lord') in the first place. Right Jonah – how's it coming on?

JONAH: Not bad . . . listen: (*He reads.*) And so it was that I sat in the fish and thanked God for sparing my life. One thought was on my mind (CARD: 'God wants me to say yes'). That was all I could think about (CARD: 'God wants me to say yes').

GOD: Everybody close your eyes and imagine you're Jonah. Let's say that again: God wants me to say yes (GOD, CARDHOLDERS, JONAH *and congregation, all together*).

TWO

GOD: Jonah, can you remember the prayer
you prayed to me when you were
inside the big fish?

JONAH: Could you jog my memory a bit?

GOD: Well . . . to start with you
remembered to call out to me in your
distress.

JONAH: At least I got something right.

GOD: Tell us the prayer then, Jonah. And
every time you say 'Oh Lord my
God' we'll all say 'How great is your
love'. Okay? (*They practise it.*) Right
start off with that. Remember this
is what Jonah prayed inside that
fish.

JONAH: Oh Lord my God . . .

ALL: How great is your love!

JONAH: In my distress, O Lord, I called to
you,
and you answered me.
From deep in the world of the dead
I cried for help, and you heard me.
You threw me down into the depths,
to the very bottom of the sea,
where the waters were all around me,
and all your mighty waves rolled over
me.
Oh Lord my God . . .

ALL: How great is your love!

JONAH: I thought I had been banished from
your presence,
And would never see your holy
temple again.
The water came over me and choked
me;
the sea covered me completely,

and seaweed was wrapped round my
head.
I went down to the very roots of the
mountains,
into the land whose gates lock shut
for ever.
But you, O Lord, brought me back
from the depths alive.
O Lord my God . . .

ALL: How great is your love!

JONAH: When I felt my life slipping away,
then, O Lord, I prayed to you,
and in your Holy Temple you heard
me.
Those who worship worthless idols
have abandoned their loyalty to you.
But I will sing praises to you;
I will offer you a sacrifice
and do what I have promised.
Salvation comes from the Lord!
O Lord my God . . .

ALL: How great is your love!

JONAH: Amen.

ALL: Amen.

THREE

GOD: I heard Jonah's prayer and told the
big fish to bring up Jonah from the
ocean depths. It took me literally and
brought up Jonah on to a beach with
a horrible noise that doesn't bear
repeating.

CARDHOLDER 1: (*looking through the cards*) I can't
find 'Burp'.

CARDHOLDER 2: I haven't got 'Belch' . . . (*They
shrug.*)

GOD: Just as well . . . Off he trudged to Nineveh to tell people to turn from their wicked ways.

JONAH: It was a long walk. Four hundred miles.

GOD: Well, it gave you time to prepare your sermon and get the seaweed out of your hair.

JONAH: It took me twenty days. Then when I got there it took me all day just to walk into the city centre, you think Nottingham's (*suitable town*) bad . . .

GOD: At long last Jonah was saying (CARD: 'Yes, Lord') and obeying me. At long last the message got through.

JONAH: I preached my heart out – I kept telling them that the Lord would destroy them if they didn't say sorry and turn from their wicked ways. And do you know what happened? . . .

GOD: The people of Nineveh prayed (CARD: 'Forgive us our sins'). It moved me to tears – it was wonderful. They all put on sackcloth . . .

JONAH: Even the cows and sheep had sackcloth on!

GOD: And they all said (CARD: 'Forgive us our sins'). They really meant it. 'Aw . . . I do love them . . .' I thought. So, I forgave them. No fire, no brimstone, no punishment. Just lots and lots of my love. (CARD: 'Aaaah . . .'. *Sigh*.)

JONAH: It was dead disappointing.

GOD: Yes, Jonah, you got quite upset

didn't you?

JONAH: Ah yes . . . couldn't we just leave the story there please?

GOD: No . . . a lot of people think it stops there but it doesn't. Come on, you'll really help all these other servants here if you tell them what happened.

JONAH: (*reluctantly*) Well . . . I was a bit put out about it.

GOD: A bit put out? You were livid with me! Go on tell them what you said. It'll help them to learn.

JONAH: Oh . . . Okay then. 'Listen here, God! Didn't I tell you all this would happen? That's why I did my best to nip off to Spain, but you wouldn't let me. I knew you would go and rotten-well forgive them. You're so rotten-well merciful and kind and loving it makes me spit. What a waste of time, I might as well be dead!' Or words to that effect. Sorry. Sounds awful now.

GOD: You see Jonah thought, 'The Lord will do things (CARD: 'My way').' Didn't you? (JONAH *nods sadly*.) It's a hard lesson to learn. So I helped Jonah because I loved him. (JONAH *sighs audibly*.) And I still do!

JONAH: (*chirpy*) Oh good!

GOD: Jonah sat looking out over Nineveh.

JONAH: The sun was blistering hot (CARD: 'Phew!').

GOD: So I made a big grapevine grow to give Jonah some shade. (*She gets everyone to hold up one arm with the hand drooping over at the top like a frond*.)

JONAH: That was really (CARD: 'Cool').

GOD: Then I sent a little worm to eat the grapevine. (*She gets everyone to make a wriggly worm with a finger of the other hand.* CARD: 'Nibble nibble'. *She gets them to tickle their own armpits.*) And the grapevine died. (*Arms all wither down.*)

JONAH: Then it turned *really* hot. And when I say hot.

GOD: I mean hot! Jonah got angry with me all over again.

JONAH: Oh no! I really liked that vine. Now it's dead and I might as well be dead too. What a life!

GOD: Can you remember what I said Jonah?

JONAH: I'll never forget it. Er . . . remind me.

GOD: 'Why should you care . . .'

JONAH: Oh yes: 'Why should you care about a vine that you didn't even grow?'

GOD: That's right and don't you think I cared for the thousands of children in Nineveh? (CARD: 'Yes Lord'.) Don't you think I know my servants through and through? (CARD: 'Yes Lord'.) Hands up if you want to serve God. Put your hand up if you think you're sometimes like Jonah. (*Hopefully they all do.*) When you put your hands up, you surrender. (*Pause.*)

JONAH: (*also with hands up*) Here are my hands, Lord, work through me. All we have to say is: Make me a servant. It might help to close your eyes like I had to. Keep your hands up; let's

pray that again, all together: make
me a servant. (*Repeat as necessary.*)
Amen.

ALL: Amen.

© Steve Stickley 1985

A RIPPING TIME

A mini-trilogy based on events found in Daniel chapter six. With suitable prayers and songs in between the acts, this could form the backbone of a family service. It is a good idea to have only one item between the acts; it is also a good idea to employ the actors to be involved in these wherever possible. (E.g. whoever is the guitarist for the final song in the play could lead a different, pertinent song between Acts I and II). Items of costume need only be superficial – a crown for the KING, a multicoloured scarf for DANIEL and black balaclavas for CRINGE and GROVEL.

A word of warning: it is easy for this to turn into the 'Cringe and Grovel Show'. Much attention must be given to the characters of DANIEL and the KING; in fact your most competent actor should play DANIEL in order to redress the balance. (Note that it is always easier to make a baddie interesting than it is to make a goodie interesting.) *A Ripping Time* has also proved successful in junior schools.

CHARACTERS: in order of acceptance.

DANIEL – The 'hero'. Full of get-up-and-go. Only just tolerates CRINGE and GROVEL.

GRANDMA WRINKLECHIN – An old but sprightly narrator.

KING – Could be King Darius. A weak-willed fellow!

CRINGE & GROVEL – The King's advisers and sycophants (the baddies). They enter and exit performing a

rhythmical walk/dance which the two
actors have devised together.

ACT I

Chair SR *with map on it. Screen or flats* USC *with entrances*
USL *and* USR.
(*Enter* GRANDMA WRINKLECHIN.)

GRANDMA W: Hello everybody, and welcome to
you all.
My name is Grandma Wrinklechin
and I'm knitting a new shawl.
I'm waiting for the King to come,
you'll meet him if you stay,
And Cringe, Grovel, Daniel, too, are
coming here today.
(*Sits on chair and watches. Enter*
DANIEL USL *followed by* CRINGE USL
and GROVEL USR *who both prance in*
step. DANIEL *and* CRINGE *arrive* DSL,
GROVEL DSR.)

CRINGE & GROVEL: (*in unison, as if blowing trumpets*)
Da-dadada-da-da-daaaa!

DANIEL: Long live the King! (*He gets the*
audience to join in with a second
proclamation.)

CRINGE & GROVEL: (*as* KING *enters, he walks* DSC *between*
them, waving) His majesty the King!
May he live for ever! Speech!
Speech! (*ad lib.*)

KING: (*clearing his throat*) Well, er . . .
hello everyone. Now . . . er . . . um,
I'd . . . er . . . like to say . . . er . . .
oh, what do I tell the people?
Cringe? Grovel?

CRINGE & GROVEL: (*sidling towards the* KING, *in unison*)

Yes, your majesty? May you live for ever!

CRINGE: Cringe!

GROVEL: Grovel! (*They cackle.*)

KING: What do I tell the people?

GROVEL: (*sarcastic*) Why don't you tell the people how you're going to solve all the problems in the kingdom.

KING: Problems? What problems?

CRINGE: (*nudging him hard*) Oh, you know. How the people in the north . . .

GROVEL: Are hungry.

CRINGE: And the people in the south . . .

GROVEL: Are thirsty.

CRINGE: And the people in the west . . .

GROVEL: Are cold.

KING: Well what about the people in the east?

CRINGE & GROVEL: They're dead! (*They cackle.*)

KING: Dead? Oh but why are they dead?

CRINGE: 'Cause they're hungry, thirsty and cold, you stupid fool!
(*All freeze.*)

GRANDMA W: (*jumping up*) The poor King has a problem,
He doesn't know how to rule,
And Cringe and Grovel try their best
To make him look a fool. (*She sits.*)

KING: (*coming forward.* CRINGE AND GROVEL *hide behind him*) I'm, er, very sorry to hear about all your problems, and I . . . er . . . intend to do something about them very soon.

CRINGE & GROVEL: How soon?

KING: As soon as I think of an idea. (*Moves* DSR.) I could . . . no . . . then there's

. . . no . . . er, even the . . . no . . .
oh, Cringe and Grovel, I need an
idea.

CRINGE & GROVEL: He needs an idea! (*They perform a
'thinking' prance in their rhythm in
opposite directions and end up
together again* CS.) We've thought of
one, your majesty, may you live for
ever! (*During the following* CRINGE
AND GROVEL *move nearer the* KING
with every phrase.)

KING: Yes?

GROVEL: Well you know the people of the
north?

CRINGE: And the south . . .

GROVEL: And the west . . .

CRINGE: And the east . . .

KING: Yes?

GROVEL: Well we think . . .

KING: Yes?

CRINGE: You ought to . . .

KING: (*exasperated*) Yes?

CRINGE & GROVEL: Shoot them! (*They laugh.*)

KING: Shoot them? Isn't that a bit cruel?

GROVEL: Yeah, but it's good fun though, innit!
(*They laugh again.*)

KING: Daniel! What do *you* think? (CRINGE
AND GROVEL *stop laughing and look
daggers at* DANIEL.)

DANIEL: (*moving in from* SL *where he has been
waiting almost patiently*) I think it's a
stupid idea, your majesty! If you
kill all the people you'd have no one
left to rule! (*All freeze.*)

GRANDMA W: (*popping up*) Daniel is quite new
here,
But he's quickly made his name,
Working hard and talking straight,

That's how he came to fame. (*She sits.*)

DANIEL: No! I think I've got a much better idea, your majesty. Have you got a map?

KING: Yes there should be one around . . . (GRANDMA W *hands him a map.*) Ah yes! Here we are.

DANIEL: (*taking map; with air of authority*) Great! Right! Cringe and Grovel come and hold this map will you.

CRINGE & GROVEL: Oh Daniel, we hate him . . . telling us what to do . . . (*General ad lib. Murmurs of hatred. They hold the map one each side and their heads follow* DANIEL's *finger throughout.*)

DANIEL: (*standing left of map*) Now, the people of the north . . . (*Points.*)

KING: (*standing right of map*) They're hungry.

DANIEL: And the people of the south . . . (*Points.*)

KING: They're thirsty.

DANIEL: And the people of the west . . . (*Points.*)

KING: They're the ones that are cold.

DANIEL: Right! So it's easy then . . . (*Should be quite fast as he points throughout.*) We take food from the south and take it to the north, then we take drink from the north and take it to the south, then we take warm clothes from the north and south and take them to the west. (CRINGE AND GROVEL *are dizzy with all the head turning.*)

KING: (*confused*) It seems very complicated, Daniel . . .

DANIEL: Oh, it's really a very simple idea,

your majesty.

GROVEL: (*seizing the opportunity*) Oh, I see,
your majesty, may you live for ever
(*letting go of the map,* CRINGE *rolls it
up*) – what you want is someone to
organise things.

CRINGE: (*not to be outdone*) Yes, your
majesty, may you live for ever. What
you need is a leader.

GROVEL: Tell you what . . . (*snatching map*)
I'll be the leader!

CRINGE: (*snatching map*) *I'll* be the leader!

GROVEL: (*snatching map*) *I* will!

CRINGE: (*snatching map*) *I* will!

GROVEL: (*snatching map*) *I* will!

KING: (*snatching map*) Daniel will! (*Hands
map to* DANIEL.)

DANIEL: (*brusque*) Very good, your majesty.
(KING *exits.*) Right, Cringe and
Grovel come over here. (*Moves* DSL
CRINGE AND GROVEL *move over and
stand each side of him moaning and
complaining.*) Now then (*opens
map*), we're going to go to the south,
get plenty of food –

GROVEL: And stuff ourselves silly till we're
sick!

DANIEL: No we won't! Then we'll go to the
north, get plenty of drink –

CRINGE: And all have a booze-up and get
drunk!

DANIEL: No we won't! Then we'll go to the
north and south, get plenty of warm
clothing –

GROVEL: And sell them to the west at great
profit and get stinking rich!

DANIEL: No we won't! Look, who are we
supposed to be helping in all this?

CRINGE & GROVEL: Ourselves! (*They cackle again.*)

DANIEL: You two are nothing but a pair of crooks. (*Hits* CRINGE AND GROVEL *respectively over the head with the rolled-up map.*) You think of no one but yourselves. (*Hits them again.*) And if you won't help, then I'll have to do it myself! (CRINGE AND GROVEL *go to protect their heads;* DANIEL *walks* USC. *They think he's gone and so relax, but he returns and hits them again.* DANIEL *exits.* CRINGE AND GROVEL *freeze.*)

GRANDMA W: (*rising*) Daniel will not work with crooks,
He's different from the rest,
He's honest, good, tells the truth,
And always does his best. (*She sits.*)

GROVEL: Here, Cringe (*both moving* SC).

CRINGE: What is it, Grovel?

GROVEL: I think we're going to have to get rid of Daniel.

CRINGE: Yeah – now, if we were to get him into trouble with the King . . .

GROVEL: Yes! Now, let's see, what's he done wrong? (*They 'think' – more idiosyncratic moves may be devised for the following.*) Is he a liar?

CRINGE & GROVEL: Mmmm? – No!

CRINGE: Has he ever stolen anything?

CRINGE & GROVEL: Mmmm? – No!

GROVEL: Is he a tell-tale?

CRINGE & GROVEL: Mmmm? – No!

CRINGE: Does he pick his nose?

CRINGE & GROVEL: Mmmmm? – No! (*They are getting angry.*)

GROVEL: Daniel hasn't done *anything* wrong!

CRINGE: Nothing at all!

CRINGE & GROVEL: Rats! (*They turn and prance as if to exit* US. *They freeze.*)
GRANDMA W: (*rising*) If you are a Christian,
Then this is what you do,
Let no one say you do things wrong,
Stand up for what is true!
(*Exeunt.*)

ACT II

(*Enter* GRANDMA WRINKLECHIN.)
GRANDMA W: There's trouble brewing in the air,
Let's see what happens now.
Cringe and Grovel hatch a plot
That's bound to start a row. (*Sits.*)
(CRINGE AND GROVEL *enter as before and move* DSC.)
CRINGE & GROVEL: (*conniving*) We've thought of a way to get rid of Daniel.
GROVEL: Once . . .
CRINGE: . . . and for all! (*Both laugh.*) He prays every morning.
GROVEL: We've seen him in his window.
CRINGE: So we thought if we got the King . . .
GROVEL: To make praying against the law . . .
CRINGE: (*turning mean*) Then we've got Daniel!
GROVEL: Once . . .
CRINGE: . . . and for all! (*They laugh.*)
KING: (*entering and walking* DS) Ah! Morning Cringe and Grovel!
CRINGE & GROVEL: (*sycophantic again*) Morning, your majesty, may you live for ever.
CRINGE: Cringe!
GROVEL: Grovel! (*They laugh.*)
CRINGE: Your majesty . . . we think it's about time you made a new law.

KING: Oh yes, that's a very good idea. I haven't made a new law for ages –

GROVEL: And it just so happens that your loyal subjects Cringe and myself have thought of a good one.

CRINGE: A very good one. (*They can hardly contain their excitement.*)

KING: Oh, well, shall I make a speech?

CRINGE & GROVEL: Yes! (CRINGE *lifts the* KING *while* GROVEL *pushes* GRANDMA W *off her chair with an apt insult and places it* CS. KING *is placed on it,* CRINGE AND GROVEL *move in front of the chair and mime trumpets again.*)
Da-dadada-da-da-da-daaa! His Majesty the King! May he live for ever! (*They retreat behind the* KING, *holding one arm each, heads poking out.*)

KING: Now, it's about time I made a law, and this law is about . . . er . . . um . . . it's about . . . er . . . oh, Cringe and Grovel – what's the law about?

CRINGE: (*stage whisper in his ear*) This is a law . . .

KING: This is a law . . .

GROVEL: (*doing the same*) That no one should pray . . .

KING: That no one should pray . . .

CRINGE: (*whispering*) And if they do . . .

KING: And if they do . . .

GROVEL: They will be thrown to the lions . . .

KING: They will be thrown to the lions . . . (*dismayed*) er . . . the lions?

CRINGE & GROVEL: (*both heads forward. With glee*) The lions!

CRINGE: This is a special law . . .

KING: This is a special law . . .

GROVEL: Which can never, never be
changed . . .

KING: Which can never, never be changed.

CRINGE & GROVEL: (*coming in front of* KING, *clapping politely*) Oh, well done your majesty!

GROVEL: How Araldite.

CRINGE: Didn't he do well . . . (*They laugh.*)

KING: (*during this speech* CRINGE AND GROVEL *stop laughing, slowly look at each other, then at the* KING, *each other, the audience, and then push the* KING *off the chair backwards.*) Now, while you're all gathered, I'd like to say something about the sewers – now they're getting very pongy lately, and I think something ought to be done . . . (*He disappears downwards and exits.*)

GROVEL: Got him! (*They laugh and move* SL *murmuring with delight.* DANIEL *enters, kneels on chair and adopts praying position. They freeze.*)

GRANDMA W: (*rising*) Daniel's got a problem,
He's going to have to choose.
If he doesn't stop his chats with God
His life he's going to lose. (*She sits.* CRINGE AND GROVEL *look silently at* DANIEL.)

DANIEL: (*praying*) Hello Father, it's me, Daniel again. They've said I must stop talking to you, but I know I can't do that – sometimes it's very hard being a Christian . . . (CRINGE AND GROVEL *tiptoe across and kneel one on each side of the chair.*) Amen. (*Breathes sigh of relief, opens eyes and sits back.*)

CRINGE & GROVEL: Boo! (DANIEL *starts with surprise*

back up to kneeling.)

CRINGE: Praying were we?

GROVEL: Having a little talk with the Lord, were we?

CRINGE & GROVEL: Oh King! (KING *enters and moves* DSC.)

KING: Yes . . . I . . . (CRINGE AND GROVEL *grab him and hurry him across to* SL.)

CRINGE: You know that law . . .

GROVEL: The one about praying . . .

CRINGE: Well we've found someone . . .

GROVEL: Who's broken it!

KING: Who?

CRINGE & GROVEL: (*pointing*) Him!

KING: Daniel? (*Moves to him.*) Is this true, have you really broken my law?

DANIEL: Listen, your majesty. (*Puts his arm round the* KING'*s shoulder and moves* SR.) How would you feel if I stopped talking to you?

KING: Oh, well, I don't think I'd like that at all.

DANIEL: My God is the greatest King of them all. I can't stop speaking to him for anyone.

KING: But I've made a law, Daniel, and you've broken it – so you must be punished.

DANIEL: But I can't stop speaking to my God!

KING: Oh dear, this is a problem. (*Moves* CS.) Cringe and Grovel, what should I do?

CRINGE & GROVEL: (*moving across to 'capture'* DANIEL) Throw him to the lions!

KING: Surely we can make an exception just this once.

CRINGE: No! This is a special law!

GROVEL: Which can never, never be changed!

(*They are delighted.*)

KING: Well, surely if your God is so great, Daniel, he'll save you from those lions, won't he?

CRINGE & GROVEL: Off to the lions! (*They take* DANIEL *towards* SR, *then move* USL, *double back and freeze* USC.)

GRANDMA W: (*takes back her chair with an ad lib. comment*)
Cringe and Grovel drag him off,
The lions lick their lips,
The King can do nothing to save him now.
Has Daniel had his chips? (*Sits.*)

CRINGE & GROVEL: Here we are at the lions! (CRINGE *mimes opening door* – CRINGE AND GROVEL *roar when it opens and stop when it shuts.*)

CRINGE: (*shutting door*) Oh dear – they look hungry, Daniel!

GROVEL: Oh, do you know what, Daniel? I forgot to give them their Kit-E-Kat this morning.

CRINGE: Never mind, they've got you instead. (*He opens door again – with roars – they're just about to throw* DANIEL *in when the* KING *leaps across and shuts the door. The roars stop.*)

KING: I've decided to give you a second chance, Daniel!

DANIEL: Oh great. (*Steps forward.* CRINGE AND GROVEL *drag him back.*)

KING: All you have to do is forget all this God business, and we'll all go home and have a cup of tea.

DANIEL: But I've told you, your majesty, I can't give up talking to God.

KING: Well, what are you going to do then?

DANIEL: I'll just have to . . . pray.

CRINGE: He did it again!

GROVEL: He broke the law!

CRINGE: 'Scuse me. (*Pushes* KING US, *opens the door and* DANIEL *is thrown in, doors shut. The* KING *has retreated off* US.)

GROVEL: (*rubbing hands gleefully*) Here, Cringe.

CRINGE: What is it Grovel?

GROVEL: I bet Daniel will have a ripping time! (*They laugh, mimic lions and exeunt taunting* GRANDMA WRINKLECHIN *with roars, etc.*)

GRANDMA W: (*on her feet*) When it's hard to be a Christian,
When people laugh at you.
Think of how Daniel stood the test,
And all that he went through. (*Exit.*)

ACT III

(DANIEL *lies down in* 'Lions Den', MSL. KING *moves DSC and freezes, worried.*)

GRANDMA W: (*entering*) The King is most upset,
He dreams of lions all night.
He hopes when they try to eat Daniel,
That God will help him fight. (*Sits.*)

KING: Ooh, I've had a terrible night. I dreamt of great horrible, ferocious lions – I almost felt like . . . praying – oh, but that's against the new law I've made. I'd better go and see if Daniel's God has saved him. (*Moves towards the door of the den.*) Daniel? Daniel? (*Jumps to try and see in a high window in the door.*) Oh I can't

see in; this window's too high.
(*Calling*) Daniel! Daniel! (*Pause, sorrowing.*) Oh, he's dead! (*He sobs long and loud.* DANIEL *snores in between sobs.* KING *cries – this goes on for two or three alternate crescendos – until the* KING *hears a snore.*) Daniel? Is that you, Daniel? Wake up, Daniel! (DANIEL *carries on snoring. The* KING *gets the audience to join him in calling* 'Wake up Daniel'.)

DANIEL: (*getting up*) I thought I heard something (*throughout the following, they look through a 'window' about one foot higher than their heads.*)

KING: Daniel, you're alive!

DANIEL: Yes, I've had a great night – I slept really well! I don't think the lions did though . . .

KING: Why's that?

DANIEL: I tend to snore a little bit.

KING: Oh, Daniel's alive, hooray! (*Dances joyfully.*)

DANIEL: Your majesty . . .

KING: (*continuing to celebrate*) His God's saved him from the lions, hooray!

DANIEL: Your majesty!

KING: (*getting carried away*) This praying stuff must really work!

DANIEL: Your majesty!

KING: Yes?

DANIEL: Would you mind letting me out, please?

KING: Oh, yes (*Moves across to let* DANIEL *out. We hear more celebrating, laughs and cries of* 'Happy Day! Oh Happy Day!' *As* CRINGE AND GROVEL *enter.*)

GROVEL: (*laughing*) 'Ere, Cringe . . .

CRINGE: What, Grovel?

GROVEL: I bet by now those horrible fierce lions will have torn Daniel limb from limb! (*They laugh.*)

CRINGE: Yeah, I bet you could say he was pretty 'armless'. (*Laughs.*)

GROVEL: Or even that he'd lost his head! (*More laughter.*)

CRINGE: I bet he hasn't got a leg to stand on! (*They are now helpless with laughter.*)

KING: (*moving across to* CRINGE AND GROVEL *with* DANIEL *in front of him*) Look you two, it's Daniel!

CRINGE & GROVEL: (*still laughing they turn their heads towards* DANIEL) Hello, Daniel. (*They carry on laughing. Stop, double take. Then aghast.*) Huh?

DANIEL: (*moving across in front of them relishing the moment*) You didn't expect to see me again did you? But I prayed to my God, and he saved me from those lions.

CRINGE & GROVEL: Get him! (*They grab him and begin to move him towards the den.*)

KING: What are you doing?

CRINGE: It didn't work the first time . . .

GROVEL: So we're going to give the lions another chance!

KING: You can't do that!

CRINGE: Oh yes we can . . .

GROVEL: We passed that law about praying.

KING: *I* passed that law.

CRINGE: No you didn't, *we* did.

GROVEL: To get rid of Daniel.

CRINGE: Goody goody!

GROVEL: Little creep!

KING: (*confused*) To get rid of Daniel?

CRINGE:	(*to* KING) Yeah, don't you understand anything?
GROVEL:	(*to* KING) Stupid idiot.
CRINGE:	Wet dishcloth.
GROVEL:	Great twit!
CRINGE:	Soppy cissy!
GROVEL:	Pathetic –
CRINGE & GROVEL:	Useless King! (*They realise their mistake, put their hands over their mouths in horror.*)
KING:	Wh . . . wh . . . WHAT?! (*All freeze.*)
GRANDMA W:	(*laughing*) At last these two have been found out, No mercy they will find. Cringe and grovel though they may, The King won't change his mind!
KING:	Useless King? There's only one thing for it! (DANIEL *shakes himself free from* CRINGE AND GROVEL'S *grip.*) To the lions! (*They both beg on their knees.*)
CRINGE:	No!
GROVEL:	Mercy!
CRINGE & GROVEL:	May you live for ever, may you live for ever, may you live for ever. Cringe, grovel (*Ad lib. until . . .*)
KING:	It's no use cringing and grovelling! (*Opens door; he and* DANIEL *provide the roars.* CRINGE *is kicked in,* GROVEL *makes a dash, but* DANIEL *grabs him and throws him in too. They scream and shout and gradually die, clinging on to each other, their death must be amusingly melodramatic.*) Daniel you still haven't told me how you survived the night.
DANIEL:	Well, I prayed to my God, and He

made those lions as harmless as little kittens; in fact they made very nice pillows to lie on. (*Realises his joke*.) Lie on! . . . never mind.

KING: Your God sounds really great, I'd like to get to know him a lot more, I think my people should too. (*Indicates audience*.) I know, I'll make a *new* law.

DANIEL: What sort of law?

KING: A law about God!

DANIEL: Great! That sounds like a cue for a song!
(CRINGE AND GROVEL *slip off their costumes and join in the song. The* KING *stands on the chair. They all start clicking their fingers as* DANIEL *or one of the cast picks up the guitar and plays. The audience are encouraged to join in the rhythm*.)

GRANDMA W: (*moving to join them*) Yahoo! About time too, music in my soul baby. Rock on Danny boy! Bop shoo loo ba loo wah!

KING: Listen everybody, let the trumpet blow.
This God is the greatest and everyone should know . . . that

ALL: God is the greatest, tell everyone.
God is the greatest, tell everyone.
God is the greatest, tell everyone that
God is the greatest King of all!

DANIEL: If you pray and ask him, he'll answer straight away.
He'll save you from your troubles; just talk to him each day . . .

GUITARIST: Two, three, four . . .

ALL: God is the greatest tell everyone.
God is the greatest tell everyone.
God is the greatest tell everyone that
God is the greatest King of all!

KING: God is the greatest King of them all
. . . (*He jumps off the chair. As he
lands:*).

ALL: Yeah!

A RIPPING TIME

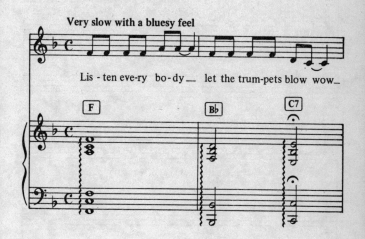

ii Adult

WODGER SAY?

This cheeky little number could be used alongside a talk or sermon either on the Holy Spirit or on Prayer. It is intended to move quite fast and is very tongue-in-cheek.

CHARACTERS: TRIFFIC TERRY – A very enthusiastic, naïve, bespectacled wimp.
ONE – Female. In obvious control of the sketch.
TWO – Male. A little unwilling. Thinks he always gets the rotten parts.

Chair USC *with a colourful cloak draped over it.* ONE *and* TWO *stand* SR *and* SL *respectively, either side of* TRIFFIC TERRY, *who stands* CS *with his back to the audience.*

ONE: Once upon a time there was a magician called Terry. Triffic Terry.

TWO: (*holding up a large sign saying 'Kapow!' in front of* TRIFFIC TERRY) Kapow!

TERRY: (*looking out from behind the sign*) Hello.

ONE: He wanted to change things.

TERRY: (*emerging from behind the sign*) I want to change things. (TWO *puts sign down.*)

ONE: But he wasn't much of a magician.

TERRY: Wodger mean not much of a

magician? I've got a magic wand. (*He
holds a wand up.*) I'll show you, I'll
change you into a septic toadstool.
Zap!

ONE: See what I mean?

TERRY: Zap! Zap!

ONE: Having a magic wand doesn't make
you a magician.

TERRY: Doesn't it? I'll show you. I'll make a
dog talk. (*Aside to* TWO.) Be a dog.
(*Smiles at* ONE.)

TWO: What?

TERRY: (*stage whisper*) Be a dog. (TWO *takes
up 'dog' position. If sightlines are bad
he could remain standing in a begging
pose.*) Dog talk! Zap!

TWO: What do you want me to say?

TERRY: There you are. It talked.

ONE: He was a fraud.

TERRY: (*to* AUDIENCE) I'm a failure.

TWO: He was going through a bad spell.

TERRY: None of my spells ever works. I can't
change anything. It's not fair. Other
magicians can do it. Why can't I?

ONE: Poor old Terry. Aah! One day a fairy
flitted in through his window to cheer
him up. Alan . . . (*or actor's name*)
. . . you're a fairy.

TWO: Pardon? (*Pause, uncomfortable
realisation.*) Oh . . . I see . . .

ONE: (*explaining*) In the story . . . Flit in
and cheer him up.

TWO: Oh flippin' heck. (*He takes up a fairy
pose but speaks without emotion as he
'Tippie-toes' across to* TERRY.) Flit flit
flit. Flit flit flit. Flit. Hello.

TERRY: Who are you?

TWO: I'm a fairy.

TERRY: (*looking him up and down*) Fairy
nuff.

TWO: What's up with you then?

TERRY: None of my spells ever works. I can't
change anything.

TWO: What you need is power. Flit flit flit.
Flit flit flit. (*He moves to chair and
stands back to audience.*)

TERRY: That's it! I need power. But I haven't
got any power. It's not fair. I want
power! I want power! Fair dos for
magicians called Terry! I want
power!

ONE: (*coughs to interrupt*) Haven't you
ever thought of asking for it?

TERRY: For what?

ONE: For power. To change things.

TERRY: Of course! I could ask the great and
mighty Wodge who lives in the
mountains above the clouds. The
overseer of all magicians! The source
of all power! (TWO *gets up on chair
having donned the cloak.*) Yeah, I'll
ask him. (*Singing.*) I'm off to see the
wizard, the wonderful wizard of
Wodge. (*He half-walks half-dances
round in a circle back to the chair.*)

TWO: I am Wodge the mighty
I am Wodge the bold.
No mortal dare approach me . . .
(*He sounds 'Bunged-up'.*)
Because I've got a cold. (*Blows his
nose in handkerchief.*)

ONE: You can't say that!

TWO: Why not?

ONE: You're supposed to be God.

TWO: Am I? Oh . . . sorry.

ONE: So Triffic Terry approaches the great

door of the palace of Wodge.

TERRY: (*miming knocking*) Knock knock.

TWO: Who's there?

TERRY: Wodge?

TWO: Wodger want?

TERRY: I want power to change things.

TWO: *You're* asking for it . . .

TERRY: Course I am, why do you think I climbed this bloomin' mountain? I want power to change things.

TWO: Like what?

TERRY: Like . . . er . . . (*He thinks briefly.*) . . . my clothes! Yeah, I want to have a huge black cloak with glittery stuff on so I can be like a real magician. I want to impress people. I want to be better than Paul Daniels – they're gonna like that . . . not a lot. (*Laughs.*) Yeah! I want people to come from miles around to see Triffic Terry doing his spells. What do you say, Wodgie?

TWO: Sorry, power's off. (*He gets down.*)

ONE: Hang on, you're supposed to answer him.

TWO: Oh . . . sorry. (*He gets back up, goes to speak but stops.*) What do I say?

ONE: (*aside*) He's got no idea! (To TWO.) Something like . . . (*She is searching for the words.*) If you don't think to ask me I can't give you my treasure . . . er . . . (*remembering*) And I may not give you anything If it's only for your pleasure. Right?

TWO: (*repeats half to self*) . . . I may not give you anything . . .

ONE: . . . If it's only for your pleasure. Right?

TWO: . . . only for your pleasure. Right.
(*Clears throat. Looks at* TERRY,
fumbling to remember.) . . . er . . .
(*matter of fact*) What she said. (*Gets
down.* ONE *tuts and sighs. They begin
to exit together.*) Well, I thought you
were great as the narrator.

ONE: I really didn't like the way you played
God.

TWO: But some people treat him like that.
The Great Eternal Benefactor
dishing out goodies . . .
(*They are about to exeunt together in
deep discussion, leaving* TERRY
nonplussed.)

TERRY: Oi!

ONE ⎫
TWO ⎭ : (*turning*) Mmmm?

TERRY: But what about me? What about my
power? And what about the
punchline?

ONE: That's for you to work out. (*Exeunt.*)

TERRY: (*sarcastic*) Oh triffic. (*Sees audience,
panic in his eyes.*) Urm . . . well . . .
you'll just have to think up a
punchline yourselves. (*Remembers
his wand.*) Ready? One, two, three
. . . Zap! (*Pause. He puts his fingers
to his temples.*) Come on, think
harder! (*Pause.*) Yes . . . I think I've
got it . . .
I thought Wodge would bestow on
me
fame, success and wealth (*Pause.*)
But then you don't receive God's
power
if it's only for . . .
(*Pause. He is stuck. He begins to*

mutter to himself as he exits.)
What on earth rhymes with wealth?
Elf? Shelf?
(*He exits bemused.*)

Note: *If children are present they may shout out the answer, in which case Terry repeats it and reponds with 'Magic!' then exits happily.*

QUENCHING THE THIRST

It is easy to perform this badly. Attention must be given to the NARRATOR's portrayal of Jesus so that it does not appear wooden or sentimental. Similarly the REFUGEE should be able to show genuine weakness and helplessness without histrionics. Generally it is best to underplay this piece as it will help to make it all the more powerful. The pace should be gentle and slow without appearing to be on the verge of grinding to a halt. If church sightlines are good, 'Quenching the Thirst' can prove very poignant in a worship setting.

Our thanks to members of 'Making Tracks' Summer School, Bolton, 1980.

> CHARACTERS: REFUGEE
> NARRATOR
> GERALD

REFUGEE *is curled up on the floor* DSR, *a chair* SL. NARRATOR *stands* USC. GERALD USL *with back to audience. He mimes the following*.

> NARRATOR: Gerald arrives home from the office. Hangs up his coat and sits down to his evening meal. (GERALD *sits in chair*.) He takes a sip of his wine. 'Mm, goes so well with pork.' He finishes his dinner and takes his wine to a comfortable chair. (*Leans back in chair. We see his reactions to the following*.) He heaves a sigh of relief and reaches for the evening paper.

He reads, 'Old people die of hypothermia in Liverpool slums.' 'Will Bolton beat Arsenal to reach the next round of the FA Cup?' 'Big pools win: two and a half million!' 'Millions starving in Ethiopia (*or topical reference*). Red Cross officials say famine relief fund is nearly empty. There is simply not enough food to go round.' (REFUGEE *has stirred. She crawls to* GERALD, *with imagined bowl, begging.* GERALD *stares uncomfortably, then turns away slightly.* NARRATOR *positions hands as if crucified.*) I am thirsty. (*Pause.* GERALD *and* REFUGEE *look at him.* REFUGEE *scoops up 'water' and crawls to* NARRATOR'S *feet.* GERALD *picks up his glass of wine and kneels reverentially at* NARRATOR'S *feet, thus forming a triangle. They both offer their drink.* NARRATOR *takes bowl and drinks. He looks at* GERALD. GERALD *looks at* REFUGEE *then offers her his wine. Pause.*) And if any of you gives a drink to any of these my little ones, because you are my disciple, I tell you the truth: you will not lose your reward. (*Pause.*)

GOD-SAND

This monologue is more of a chat. It should convey a friendly relaxed approach without being slapdash; in fact a director could be invaluable here. 'God-sand' could prove a God-send in a service where God's promises are being explored or perhaps where we are called to examine our own faithfulness.

CHARACTER: ABRAHAM – has an infectious laugh. A very affable, sprightly gent. Wears a black hat and carries a calculator and tweezers.

ABRAHAM: (*He is counting grains of sand with tweezers and moves them from an imaginary pile on his right to one on his left.*) . . . *six, seven, eight, nine, ten.*

That makes (*consults calculator*) nine hundred billion, four hundred million, two hundred and fifty thousand, one hundred and sixty. Phew. (*Resumes counting.*) One, two, three. (*Notices audience.*) Oh. Didn't see you there. Hang on a minute . . . four, five, six, seven, eight, nine, ten. That's . . . (*calculator again*) good. Hello, sorry about that. I know what you're thinking – I've lost my marbles. (*Laughs.*) Grains of sand

maybe, but marbles . . . no. Have
you ever tried counting grains of
sand? They are so small, you see, or
rather you can't see, they're so
difficult to see, you see. (*Picks one
up.*) I'm moving all this sand in this
pile here, to that pile there. Using
these. (*Holds up tweezers.*) I know
what you're thinking – what's wrong
with a shovel . . . a bulldozer even?
(*Laughs.*) If only I could. But I
couldn't keep count, could I? I mean,
have you ever sat on a beach with a
handful of sand (*he mimes grabbing
a handful and allows it to trickle out*)
wondering how many grains there
are? (*Looks at hand.*) Mind you, it
depends on the size of your hand,
doesn't it? I know what you're
thinking – why am I counting grains
of sand? (*Pause.*) Oh you're not
thinking that, well in that case . . .
(*goes on counting*) I'm going to tell
you anyway. (*Laughs.*) You see I was
going to count the stars but you can
only see them at night, and then only
when it's a clear sky – besides which
I'll probably get a stiff neck looking
up for so long. So sand is infinitely
better. (*Laughs.*) Infinitely . . . Oh
yes, that's the whole point. You see I
said to my wife . . . (*Laughs.*) You
should meet Sarah; you'd like her I
know you would. Anyway, I told her
we were going to have a baby.
Normally the wife tells the husband,
but no matter (*laughs*) and that we
should have a huge family. (*Laughs.*)

It wasn't my idea. (*Laughs*.) It was
God's idea. (*Laughs*.) Oh dear
(*pause*) oh I'm sorry you don't know
what I'm laughing at do you? You
see the point was, at the time I was
ninety-nine years old and I'd lost my
get-up-and-go and Sarah, well, hers
had got up and gone! (*Laughs*.) We
gave up sex along with all the other
athletic pursuits like running up and
down the stairs . . . Anyway . . . we
had a son. And do you know what we
called him? (*Laughs*.) 'Laughing'!
(*Laughs*.) That was his name,
'Laughing' (*He calms down*.)
Anyway, most people get a telegram
from the Queen when they're a
hundred; I got a baby boy! (*Laughs*.)
It was all God's plan you see – he
certainly doesn't do things by halves,
eh? 'Abraham', he said, 'you shall
have as many descendants as there
are stars in the sky', he said. 'Or
grains of sand on the beach', I said.
At first I used to lie awake at night
thinking about it all. I started
counting sheep but fell asleep. Sand's
much better; it can't run away. So
that's why I'm counting you see – it's
a way of saying thank you I suppose.
(*Makes as if to count again; a sudden
teasing thought crosses his mind*.) Do
you know how long it takes to count
up to one million? Hmm? Do you?
Eight weeks, one day, twenty hours,
six minutes and twenty seconds . . .
approximately. And I should know!
Oh, that's without sleep, by the way.

So at that rate you could count up to six million three hundred thousand in one year. But you'd have big bags under your eyes! (*Laughs, holds up calculator*.) I'm glad they've invented these, that's all I can say. (*Laughs. Becoming wistful*.) When I think how small, how insignificant I used to feel. Just like . . . er . . . just like a grain of sand. I had nothing. We all feel like that sometimes don't we? You know something? We might be small, but we all count. (*Pause*.) You know if I were alive today, I'd still be counting! (*Counts estimated number in audience in blocks of ten or fifty, etc*.) Fantastic! That's . . . (*suitable number*) give or take an odd one, and there's an odd one! (*Points into audience, laughs*.) That makes (*calculator again*) nine hundred billion, four hundred million, two hundred and fifty thousand (*audience number + 170*). Brilliant! (*Looks at audience*.) Your descendants will be as many as the stars. (*He turns as if to exit, then turns back quickly*.) Did you know that every hair on your head was numbered? Get your microchips round that one, eh? God bless! (*Exits playing with calculator and laughing*.)

CHURCHOPOLY

Originally inspired by Amy Carmichael's vision of the desperate need for missionaries and the Church's subsequent lack of response, this piece formed part of a presentation designed to help Christians to see the spiritual need around them. Carmichael's version gave a picture of a circle of people playing at making daisy chains while only yards away blind, helpless souls plummeted over a cliff to their death. Churchopoly could be used in a situation where teaching is being given about the Christian's responsibility to those around him who have never heard the Gospel. It is important that the characters are portrayed as larger than life, almost cartoon-like, as this will help the piece to become more unpalatable as it goes on.

CHARACTERS: CHAIRMAN – a stick-in-the-mud. Wears dog collar.

SECRETARY – attempts to be go-ahead but remains conservative. Wears a gaudy tie.

TREASURER – a Scot, tight-lipped and tight-pursed. Wears small bow tie.

YOUTH LEADER – enthusiastic wimp with large wooden cross and badge.

MISSION SECRETARY – very well-meaning busybody. Wears large floral hat.

SET: *A chair* USC *behind a table* CS *on which are seen two large colourful (foam) dice, a large monopoly-type board folded in half and two piles of cards for 'Community Chest' and 'Chance'. On the floor* US *by the chair there are large silver models of a minister (Action Man), a pulpit, a hymn book, an offering plate and a vase of flowers.*

Enter CHAIRMAN *who sits in chair. All enter chatting and greeting each other.* CHAIRMAN *raps on table and clears his throat loudly. Immediate silence. All kneel upright, almost prayer-like, around the table leaving* DS *side visible.*

CHAIRMAN: Well, if everyone is present, we'll begin. (*He stands solemnly. He chants High-Church fashion.*) Very serious. Very properly.

ALL: (*chanting without resolving*) We are playing Churchopoly.

CHAIRMAN: (*unfolds board and puts cards into position*) Let us have the piece offering. (*He picks up the silver models and hands them to the respective people.*) There's your piece. And here is your piece. That piece is for you, this one for you. And . . . (*Picks up the Action Man minister.*) . . . this is my piece. All ready? Let's begin. (*He sits. They all chant, skipping-rhyme fashion as the* SECRETARY *shakes then rolls the dice on to the board.*)

ALL: Very serious, very properly. We are playing Churchopoly.

SECRETARY: Seven! (*He moves his pulpit.*) One, two, three, four, five, six, seven. Aah, the minutes. (*Everyone else adopts a sleeping position. He stands and rattles off like a machine-gun.*) The minutes of the last meeting were the same as the minutes of the previous meeting and will probably be the same as the minutes of this

meeting. Let us pray for the minutes.
Dear Lord, bless these minutes.
Amen. (*He kneels.*)

ALL: Amen.

CHAIRMAN: (*he has actually dropped off. He is
nudged awake*) Er . . . Amen!

ALL: (*chanting, skipping-like as before as
TREASURER rolls the dice*)
Very serious, very properly
We are playing Churchopoly.

TREASURER: Eleven! (*Moving his 'offering plate'.*)
Two, four, six, eight, ten, eleven.
Financial report. (*He stands.*) The
church steeple is still falling down.

ALL: (*disappointed*) Aah . . .

TREASURER: But the renovation fund has been
boosted by the recent church bazaar.

ALL: Hooray!

TREASURER: The tombola raised twenty-five pounds.

ALL: Hooray!

TREASURER: The women's sewing circle raised
fifty pounds.

ALL: Hooray!

TREASURER: And Madame Za-Za's crystal ball
raised a marvellous five hundred
pounds!

ALL: A-le-lu-ia!

CHAIRMAN: Marvellous report! Have an extra go.

TREASURER: (*rolls dice*) Three. One, two, three.
Praise and worship!

ALL: (*They all stand and join hands. They
sing to the tune 'hickory dickory
dock' and dance, encircling the table.*)
Happity clappity clap
Happity clappity clap. (*They change
direction.*)
Love and joy and peace and God,
Happity clappity clap. (*They assume*

*original positions and chant as before
as* YOUTH LEADER *rolls dice.*)
Very seriously, very properly
We are playing Churchopoly.

YOUTH LEADER: Thwee. (*Moves 'hymn book'.*) One,
two, thwee. Youth gwoup weport.
(*Stands enthusiastically.*) We have
seen some vewy encouraging signs.

ALL: (*encouraged*) Hmm!

YOUTH LEADER: There is a gweater level of
commitment and some new people
coming along. We are enjoying some
close fellowship.

ALL: (*still encouraged*) Hmm!

YOUTH LEADER: In fact (*he is getting excited*) . . . we
are thinking of starting a dwama
gwoup!

ALL: (*horrified*) What? A drama group?
Go to jail! (*They all point to him. He
kneels back down, crushed.*)

SECRETARY: What do you think this is? House
Churchopoly?

ALL: (*as before, as* MISSION SECRETARY *rolls
dice*)
Very serious, very properly
We are playing Churchopoly.

SECRETARY: Six! (*Counts quickly under breath as
she moves the 'vase of flowers'.*)
Missionary report. (*She stands.*)

ALL: Oh good! Lights out for slides!

SECRETARY: No slides this week . . .

ALL: (*disappointed*) Ooh!

SECRETARY: (*producing letter from pocket*) But I
do have a letter from Jenny Black in
Bongo-Bongo-land.

ALL: Oh good! (*They sit back and make
themselves comfortable.*)

SECRETARY: (*clears her throat. Reading*) Dear all,

it is the height of summer here in Bongo-Bongo-land and is extremely hot from dawn till dusk. (ALL *make envying noises*.)

CHAIRMAN: Sun tan!

SECRETARY: Which means we haven't had any rain for four months. (*Her tone becomes a little disappointed. She cheers up suddenly*.) I am in charge of lots of lovely children. (*Interrupts her own reading*.) Aah! (ALL *echo her sentiments and smile at each other*.) Most of them have malnutrition because . . . (*she is slightly embarrassed*) of lack of water . . . er . . . then it goes on a bit about . . . (*she scans the letter half audibly*) only hospital in 900 miles, volume of work increasing . . . Oh! Here's a good bit! (ALL *are eager. She continues to read*.) I managed to get away for a couple of days to visit a game park in the East.

ALL: (*ad lib. comments*) Oh ho! Lucky her! Elephants! (*etc., they are enjoying the excursion*.)

SECRETARY: (*still bright and breezy at first*) When I got back to the hospital I discovered there had been an outbreak of dysentery (*the tone is altering to awkward disappointment*) and twenty children and babies had died. (ALL *are embarrassed. She is shocked*.) Then it goes on a bit . . . er (*reading again*) I seem to be tired all the time . . . there's so much to do. (*She suddenly perks up*.) But I always think about

you and look forward to seeing you
all again! God bless you all. Jenny
Black. There. (ALL *make an attempt
at a positive hmmm! Brief silence.*)

CHAIRMAN: (*suddenly decisive*) Well I think we
ought to call her home for a nice rest!

ALL: Yes!

CHAIRMAN: Then when she's recovered . . . she
can go back again. All in favour?

ALL: Aye! (MISSION SECRETARY *is delighted;
she kneels back down.*)

CHAIRMAN: Good, that's that.

ALL: (*they all kneel again.* CHAIRMAN *rolls
dice*)
Very serious, very properly
We are playing Churchopoly

CHAIRMAN: Twelve! (*He takes an inordinately
long time to count out the numbers
with his Action Man.* ALL *get restless
and he eventually takes the hint.*)
One, two, three, four, um . . . five,
six (*looks up. Moves Action Man
on*), twelve. Ah! Community Chest.
(*He takes a card.*)

ALL: Read it out, read it out!

CHAIRMAN: (*grave expression crosses face*) Oh
dear.

ALL: Read it out, read it out!

CHAIRMAN: Start an evangelistic campaign. (ALL
groan.) Wait a minute! . . . or take a
chance!

ALL: (*excitedly*) Take a chance, take a
chance!

CHAIRMAN: Let's pray first. (*They all adopt
praying pose and mumble
incoherently, except* SECRETARY *who
half raises hands doll-like and repeats
through a fixed smile* 'Lord, Lord,

Lord' *and* CHAIRMAN *who pinches bridge of nose and pronounces with great importance.*) Mumbo jumbo. Mumbo jumbo. Mumbo . . . jumbo. Amen.

ALL: Amen.

CHAIRMAN: (*takes Chance card*) Redecorate interior of church.

ALL: Oh dear! Oh no!

CHAIRMAN: (*gravely*) We'll have to make cutbacks.

ALL: But what?

CHAIRMAN: Coffee and biscuits after morning service?

ALL: No!

TREASURER: (*standing*) The proposed new pew cushions?

ALL: No! (TREASURER *kneels back down.*)

MISSION SEC: (*standing*) We could sell the Youth Group's Space Invader machine.

ALL: No! No! (MISSION SECRETARY *kneels.*)

SECRETARY: (*standing and very tentatively looking round for approval*) Er . . . we could cut down on missionary support . . . ?

ALL: (*realising they can get away with that*) Yes, yes, yes!

CHAIRMAN: Let us pray. (*They repeat praying poses.*) Thank you, Lord, for providing in our hour of need. Amen.

ALL: Amen!
(*Rising to repeat song and dance.*)
Happity clappity clap,
Happity clappity clap
Love and joy and peace and God,
Happity clappity clap.

© Mission Control 1981

SPITLIGHT

An unusual, almost surrealistic piece when performed in the right conditions. Where there are younger teenagers present there is the danger that they may giggle towards the end. It is probably better to reserve it for an adult audience who would appreciate the change of mood and understand the breaking of conventions that the piece employs; and appreciate the menacing atmosphere. It is a good idea not to put this with 'Bad Noose, Good Noose' (p. 178) in a programme of sketches. (Parts of it evolved from 'Spitlight'.)

Our thanks to members of 'Making Tracks' Summer school, Bolton 1980.

CHARACTERS: ONE – As the bespectacled presenter he is cynical and a little sarcastic.

TWO – Basic puppeting skills an advantage.

THREE – Basic puppeting skills an advantage, but, more importantly, must have a strong stage presence.

There is a large table CS with a chair immediately US. A large purple or blue velvet cloth covers the table face down. It is a good idea to back the cloth with black fabric so that the colour is not revealed until the end. ONE sits on the chair. TWO and THREE are hidden either side of ONE, with appropriate props, half under the table. The cloth must reach the floor on all sides of the table except US edge. The puppets are made simply from white or cream long socks – the only useful features to include are the eyes.

ONE: Good evening. Tonight on Spotlight
we examine a most unsavoury topic.
Those of you with a more nervous
disposition may find some episodes in
tonight's programme rather
disturbing. The subject we look at in
close detail
is . . . spit. (*A slight pause. It is
obvious he is not happy with his lot.*)
Yes . . . spit. We approach the
subject from an historical
perspective. We begin in the Wild
West where men were men, women
were women and Apache was
something you wore on your knee.
(*Laughs uneasily at his own attempt
at humour.*) . . . sorry. The Wild
West, where men were men and
saloons had spittoons. (*He sits back
slightly as two sock puppets emerge
either side of him. He watches the
action.*)

TWO: (*on the left of* ONE) Well hello, Lucy.

THREE: (*on the right of* ONE) Oh Jake! My
hero. What have you been doing
today?

TWO: I've been out on the prairie hunting
buffalo.

THREE: (*excited*) Ooh! What happened Jake?

TWO: I was walking down a track when all
of a sudden . . . out jumped a
mountain lion! (*A piece of
lion-coloured fur appears from
underneath the table.* 'JAKE'
*frantically wrestles with it for two or
three seconds.* ONE *obviously regards
the whole episode as childish. The fur
disappears underneath again.*)

THREE: Oh Jake! My hero! Why, you could do almost anything Jake.

TWO: Sure could, Lucy. See that spittoon over there?

THREE: (*looking* SR) Yeah . . .

TWO: I bet I could hit it from thirty yards. (*He briefly summons saliva and 'spits' SR. 'LUCY' and ONE follow the imaginary projectile with their eyes. As it lands a sharp 'ching' is heard – this is provided by THREE who hits a suitable metal object under the table.*)

ONE: (*disgusted by it, pushes puppets back down*) Really! It's no wonder America's in a disgusting state today. (*Gaining composure.*) Of course, in this country things are *very* different. There was a time, regrettably, when buses and trains were compelled to display notices reading 'No standing. No smoking. No spitting.' But now, about the only place where one may still witness this revolting habit is on Match of the Day . . . (*A puppet appears on his left apparently holding a mini-microphone.*)

TWO: Here we are in the last minute of the FA Cup quarter-final between Bolton and Watford. And with the score still dead-locked at nil-nil, it's a corner to Bolton in the last few seconds. There's young Brandon Scraggins the new eighteen-year-old wonder striker who's tipped to play for England, waiting in the penalty box . . . (*The other puppet has appeared on* ONE's *right, jogging backwards and forwards.*) The corner's taken . . . floating into the middle . . . Scraggins rises and meets it in the air . . . ('SCRAGGINS' *does appropriate actions.* THREE *makes loud summoning saliva and spitting noise.*) A clean, spherical one right into the corner of the net! That takes Bolton through to the semi-finals! This young Scraggins is surely the dead spit of Kevin Keegan . . .

ONE: (*pushing both puppets back down. He is obviously getting fed up*) All right, all right, put a sock in it. Thank you. Spitting is detrimental to the welfare of our nation. It is unnecessary, undesirable, uncouth, dirty, disgusting and down right depraved. (*Realises he is losing his cool.*) Ahem . . . no good ever came out of spit.

THREE: (*puppet appears*) Yes it did.

ONE: No it didn't. (*Pushes it down.*)

THREE: (*popping up again*) Yes it did!

ONE: No it didn't! (*Pushes it down.*)

THREE: (*persisting*) Yes it did! I know a great story about a really good spit! (ONE *more or less gives up.*) But we need some more people for this. Er . . . (*Looks around then immediately down.*) Ah! (*Puppet pulls* THREE*'s head up so that his chin rests on the table.* ONE *resignedly sits back with a 'Tut'.*) Hello. (*His puppet has disappeared underneath.*) Gather round everyone. (TWO *appears in the same fashion, puppet first.*) Hello.

TWO: Hello. (*His puppet goes.*)

THREE: Rent a head! (*They both chuckle.*

ONE *shakes his head and sighs.*) Once
there was a man. Er . . . (*to* ONE) Oi!
You! (ONE *looks down.*) You can be
the man.

ONE: Er . . . right. (*He stands,
embarrassed.*)

THREE: He was blind.

ONE: (*stuck for what to do*) Er . . .

THREE: Cover your eyes with your hands or
something.

ONE: Ah, right. (*He does so.*)

THREE: Take your glasses off first!

ONE: (*removes glasses*) Er . . . right.

THREE: (*emerging from behind table to
standing* SR *his mood changes*) He
used to crawl on the ground. (ONE
*with eyes closed gropes for table then
crawls on it.* TWO *also emerges* SL.)
People used to gather round and
mock him.

TWO: (*taunting*) Blind man, blind man!
Seen any good films lately? (*Jeers.*)

THREE: One day a stranger appeared. He
really cared about him.
(*Moves to* ONE *on table who is
groping the air with one hand.*)

ONE: (*genuine pathos*) Help me . . .

THREE: Do you want to see?

ONE: More than anything.

THREE: So the stranger spat on the ground.
(*He mimes spitting on the table and
making mud. He rubs the 'mud' into*
ONE*'s eyes, who is a little shocked at
first.*)

ONE: Ah! (*Slowly feels his own eyes and
gradually opens them. He rubs the
'mud' off. His comments are played
down at first, the amazement being*

kept tightly under control.) I can
see . . . I can see. I can see the
ground. (*He jumps off the table* DS
looking around.) People, trees, the
grass. (*He allows himself to smile.*) I
can see the sky. (*Looks at* THREE) I
can see everything. (*Crosses to* THREE
but stops before he reaches him.
Pause.)

THREE: (*moving immediately* DS *of table*)
Everyone loved the stranger . . .

TWO: Miracle worker.

ONE: Wonderful healer. (*He kneels* SR *of*
THREE's *feet.*)

TWO: Lord and Master. (*He kneels* SL *of*
THREE's *feet.*)

ONE: Great teacher.

BOTH: King of the Jews! (*Their heads are*
bowed. Pause. They raise their heads
slowly; there is menace in their
voices.) King of the Jews! (*They rise*
and each takes one US *corner of the*
cloth on the table. The menace
increases.) King of the Jews! (*They*
snatch the cloth violently over their
shoulders so that it drapes in folds to
the front. Throughout this sequence
THREE's *countenance changes to show*
sadness and indignity. ONE *and* TWO
are venomous.) King of the Jews!
(*Screaming.*) Save yourself! (*They*
'spit' in his face. Stillness. Silence.
THREE *lowers his head slightly and*
slowly, but not so his face is obscured.
Another stillness.)

FOR FORM'S SAKE

Although particularly useful for adults at Christmas, this piece could also help to spark off other thoughts and insights throughout the year. God doesn't behave according to our expectations so it is refreshing, perhaps unnerving too, that our world needs to be turned on its head from time to time. It is precisely because God cannot be confined to a form that the adventure begins.

CHARACTERS: INTERVIEWER – Already at the end of her tether. Normally controlled, efficient and capable. Resorts to sarcasm only on certain days . . .

STEPHANIE – An office minion, annoyingly bouncy.

JOSEPH – An honest, no-messin' Northern woodworker. Very enthusiastic when he talks about God.

INTERVIEWER *at a desk with vacant seat in front. She pushes a buzzer. Enter* STEPHANIE.

INTERVIEWER: Send the next one in, Stephanie.

STEPHANIE: (*holding nose to give effect of Tannoy voice*) Mr Joseph to cubicle six, please. Mr Joseph to cubicle six.

INTERVIEWER: I wish you wouldn't do that, Stephanie. (*Exit* STEPHANIE. *Enter* JOSEPH.)

JOSEPH: Afternoon. This isn't going to take too long is it? Only I'm in a bit of a rush, you know how it is.

INTERVIEWER: That all depends on you, mister . . . er?

JOSEPH: Joseph. (*He sits down in vacant seat.*)

INTERVIEWER: Yes. Well Mr Joseph, for your information Bethlehem Department of Health and Census deals with an average of two thousand, three hundred people a day. Fifty per cent of these tend to be illiterate, dishonest and incapable of answering the most rudimentary questions about their personal background. So when you ask me how long this is going to take, I'm tempted to say anything between five minutes and three weeks, depending on the number of brain cells you can call upon.

JOSEPH: Aye . . . it's just I'm in a bit of a rush, you know how it is.

INTERVIEWER: Have you filled out forms S24 and MX15?

JOSEPH: The pink one and the green one?

INTERVIEWER: Precisely, the pink one and the green one.

JOSEPH: Well I had a bit of bother borrowing a pen, but I've made a start.

INTERVIEWER: Let me see please. (JOSEPH *pulls them out of his pocket, bringing clouds of woodshavings.*) Thank you. Hmm. Mr Joseph, all you have done is put your name on these.

JOSEPH: Aye . . . like I said, I made a start.

INTERVIEWER: In the box marked 'address & postcode'.

JOSEPH: Oh, the bloke next to me said that was . . .

INTERVIEWER: Let's start at the beginning shall we?

Name, Jo . . .

JOSEPH: Joseph.

INTERVIEWER: I think we've established that. Father's name?

JOSEPH: Heli, the son of Matthat, the son of Levi, the son of Melki . . .

INTERVIEWER: Just your father's name. Now your place of birth?

JOSEPH: Nazareth.

INTERVIEWER: That explains a lot. Vocation?

JOSEPH: It's in Galilee.

INTERVIEWER: What is?

JOSEPH: Nazareth. The vocation of Nazareth.

INTERVIEWER: I know where Nazareth is. I'm asking (*as if he is a foreigner*) HOW-DO-YOU-MAKE-YOUR-LIVING?

JOSEPH: (*mimics*) BY-CUTTING-UP-WOOD. I'm a carpenter in't I? A good 'un as well. You ask anyone who's got one of me tables. You take this joint for instance . . . (*He gets down under the table to look.*)

INTERVIEWER: Dependants. Have you got any . . . (*Finds he is gone and looks under the table.*) Does anyone depend on you?

JOSEPH: No. (*Pops his head up.*) My mother reckoned you could never depend on me. (*Laughs. Tails off.*) You're not the laughing type are you? (*Stands again.*)

INTERVIEWER: No dependants?

JOSEPH: None. Is that it then? Can I get back to me missus now? (*Starts to exit.*)

INTERVIEWER: The missus . . .

JOSEPH: Yes, we're expecting our first baby you see, any day now. I'm going to be a dad. (*Pause.*) 'Congratulations'

Footnotes

	– oh thanks very much.
INTERVIEWER:	Two dependants then, Mr Joseph. (*Indicates he should sit down.*) A wife and a child?
JOSEPH:	Oh aye . . . as I say the boy's due any day now and there's Mary . . .
INTERVIEWER:	Your wife.
JOSEPH:	(*reluctantly*) Fiancée.
INTERVIEWER:	Ah, now we're getting the picture. Been a little bit overeager have we, Mr Joseph? Sampled the goods before we've paid for them, hmmm?
JOSEPH:	You wouldn't understand.
INTERVIEWER:	No, I doubt if I would. We only get on with our jobs in this office. We don't have time for chasing each other round the filing cabinets or lingering embraces by the duplicator.
JOSEPH:	(*under his breath*) Perhaps you ought to start work earlier.
INTERVIEWER:	What?
JOSEPH:	I said 'perish the thought'.
INTERVIEWER:	Lucky for you, Mr Joseph, as far as the census is concerned, your little indiscretion is immaterial. All I need to record is the name of the child's parents. So, wife's name Mary did you say?
JOSEPH:	(*sitting*) Aye, Mary.
INTERVIEWER:	(*writing*) Mary, and father's name: Joseph.
JOSEPH:	Yeah . . . well . . . practically.
INTERVIEWER:	Practically . . . your name is practically Joseph.
JOSEPH:	No, my name is Joseph and I'm practically the father.
INTERVIEWER:	Excuse me . . . (*Pushes 'buzzer' on her desk.*) Stephanie dear, can you

bring me one of my red tranquillisers
to cubicle six with a glass of water?
Thank you. Now Mr Joseph if you
could be a little more specific.

JOSEPH: Aye. The thing is – I don't know if
this has to go on the census form like
– but Mary and I haven't . . . you
know, as such like.

INTERVIEWER: Haven't?

JOSEPH: You know. Contemplated the
marriage, as they say.

INTERVIEWER: Oh *consummated!*

JOSEPH: Not so loud.

INTERVIEWER: I'm with you, Mr Joseph. But since
Mary is pregnant I think we can
assume there is a father.

JOSEPH: (*conceding reluctantly*) Er . . . yes.
Sort of.

INTERVIEWER: But of course you have no idea of the
identity of this person.

JOSEPH: Oh aye. I know who it is!

INTERVIEWER: (*under strain*) Then, Mr Joseph,
reveal to me the name of your
fiancée's child's father and I can put
it on the census form, you can go
home and I can take my tranquilliser
and have a little cry before the next
person comes in. (*Pause.* JOSEPH
looks around briefly.)

JOSEPH: (*hushed tones*) God.

INTERVIEWER: God. (*Pause. Sighs heavily.*) Your
fiancée's having God's child.

JOSEPH: I know. I mean I didn't believe it at
first. Why me? A carpenter from't
North. He could've chosen the wife
of a governor or a king. But no. Isn't
that God's grace, eh? He chooses a
couple of nobodies like us.

(INTERVIEWER *begins to weep*.) I know, sometimes I'm so happy I could cry an' all. At first I couldn't believe what Mary said, but then the angel told me himself. It's like Mary says, 'you just have to be willing'.

INTERVIEWER: (*speaking through tears*) Mr Joseph, I believe this is your census form. (*Rips up the forms and throws them in the air, stands and leans over the table towards* JOSEPH.) Now I don't believe you exist! Bethlehem Department of Health and Census has never set eyes on you, and we don't know anything about your fiancée's, yours or anybody else's child. Now go home and whatever you do, don't try to register at this office again!

JOSEPH: Oh, will that be all then?

INTERVIEWER: (*hysterically*) Go!

JOSEPH: Right. (*Pausing as he exits*.) God bless, missus. (*He starts to exit. To* STEPHANIE *as she enters*.) I hope you've done your form right. She's in a funny mood. (STEPHANIE *is confused as she watches him exit*.)

INTERVIEWER: Ah, Stephanie, don't send anyone in for a while. How many more are there in the waiting room?

STEPHANIE: Oh, we've just had a load come in, miss. Three kings and a whole crowd of shepherds. I'm afraid the sheep have eaten their S24s.

ONE BODY

This is essentially a dance piece with words. The action should convey more than the words, with the TEMPTER working very hard at being convincing in a subtle way without the danger of appearing melodramatic. Before working at it, make sure everyone understands what is happening. It is a relatively simple piece to learn, but don't let that convince you that you've come to grips with it. Much attention needs to be given to the movements and also to the way in which the TEMPTER uses the word 'temptation'. (A series of exercises may be useful where members of the group try to communicate an emotion, e.g. hunger, urgency, sadness, hope, etc., using a fairly neutral word like linoleum, mountains, ocean or even dual-carriageway! Apart from providing an enjoyable game it will really help to concentrate on the nuances of intonation and stress. Substitute body movements for words to discover the dynamics involved when attempting to convey the same emotion physically. Then narrow it down to eyes only with no facial help and see if you can still succeed!)

Our grateful thanks to the members of the Young Theatre Church, Bolton, for the original idea.

> CHARACTERS: ONE – Female dancer. Small stature if possible.
> TWO – Male dancer.
> THREE – Female dancer.
> TEMPTER – Male dancer. Tall if possible. Must have strong presence.

NB Characters ONE, TWO and THREE never appear to see TEMPTER.

The three hold hands to form a circle facing outwards, CS. *On an agreed signal (squeezing of hands by one person) the circle rotates clockwise in a side-stepping rhythm so that each person is seen by the audience in one revolution. The rotation continues as they speak in the rhythm.*

ALL: (*slowly*) We are one body. We move as one.

ONE: (*faces the audience. Speaks double-time.*) We are one body. (*They rotate.*)

TWO: (*facing audience, also double-time*) We move as one. (*They rotate.*)

THREE: (*facing audience, double-time*) We are one body. (*On the word 'body' they stop rotating, leaving* THREE *facing* DS. *Enter* TEMPTER. *He moves slowly and slyly around the circle, eventually deciding to tempt* THREE. *He crosses in front of her then whispers through clenched teeth.*)

TEMPTER: (*suggesting anger*) Temptation . . . (THREE*'s face reflects her difficulty in resisting. He passes across her to her other ear. As his anger and volume increase we begin to see the emotion reflected in his body.*) Temptation?

THREE: (*summoning up courage to resist*) No! (*She turns sharply inward, letting go and then grabbing the hands of* ONE *and* TWO *again. Rebuffed, the* TEMPTER *moves* SR *as the circle rotates again until* TWO *faces* DS. TEMPTER *is subtly looking for a way into the circle. He walks round the back, ending up* SL *of* TWO.)

TEMPTER: (*suggesting greed*) Temptation . . . (TWO *shows his difficulty in resisting in his eyes and face.* TEMPTER *crosses*

SR *of* TWO. *Suggests increased greed
with a subtle gesture.*) Temptation?

TWO: (*showing determination*) No!
(*He turns quickly as* THREE *did. The
circle rotates to bring* ONE *to face* DS.
As it does so TEMPTER *moves in
opposite direction all the way round
them to* SR *of* ONE. *There is a
suggestion of annoyance in his eyes.*)

TEMPTER: (*sensual*) Temptation . . . (ONE
shows surprise, then fear. TEMPTER
smiles and crosses her to SL. *He
increases the emphasis – we see it in a
simple movement, e.g. placing his
hand sensuously on his own
shoulder.*) Temptation?

ONE: (*having great difficulty*) Er . . .
(*What happens next is extremely
quick and should take us by surprise.
As soon as* ONE *hesitates,
releasing her grip with* TWO *and*
THREE, TEMPTER *enters the circle.
Pause. We must be able to see*
TEMPTER *above the head of* ONE. *Hate
wells up in him but we only see it in
his eyes. He leans purposefully
forward to the side of* ONE'*s head. He
is facing the front but his eyes look at*
ONE.)

TEMPTER: (*half whispering into her ear*) I don't
need you. (*He moves back to the
centre of the circle, then moves
forward to the other side of* ONE'*s
head. As before, but with slightly
increased emphasis.*) I don't need you.
(*He moves back and looks over* ONE
*to the audience. During the following
his gloating increases as he catches the*

eyes of members of the audience.)

ONE: (*to* TWO) I don't need you. (*A slight ripple moves down her arm to* THREE.) I don't need you (*slight ripple again*).

TWO: (*to* ONE) I don't need you. (*Sends slight ripple back to* THREE.) I don't need you. (*Sends slight ripple.*)

THREE: (*to* TWO) I don't need you. (*The ripple is getting bigger. To* ONE) I don't need you (*ripple*).

ONE & TWO: (*to* THREE) I don't need you. (*They both ripple arms to* THREE *who is pulled slightly.*)

THREE & ONE: (*to* TWO) I don't need you! (*The rippling is becoming fierce and jarring.* TEMPTER *has broken into a smile. He seems to be swaying with the movement.*)

TWO & THREE: (*to* ONE) I don't need you! (*It has become pulling.* TEMPTER *begins to raise fists as though pushing outward on something invisible. We see the effort increasing during the following.*)

ALL THREE: (*to each other, ad lib., the rhythm broken*) I don't need you! I don't need you! etc.
(*It builds to a climax of angry shouting and pulling, jarring movements. The whole circle is distorting.* TEMPTER *eventually opens his fist into claws and with a strong gesture forces the three to break their grip. He remains in the pushing position until the end as* ONE, TWO *and* THREE *fall away from the centre as if to fall to the floor, but stopping before complete collapse in disjointed,*

disfigured and helpless positions.
Their bodies ripple and bounce very
slightly after the 'explosion',
eventually coming to a stillness.
Silence. TEMPTER *smiles victoriously.*
Pause.)

SECTION 2 – MUSICAL

Mr G

This version of the Tenants in the Vineyard (Matt. 21: 33–46 and Luke 20: 9–19) needs exhaustive and exhausting rehearsal. It is not worth attempting this piece if actors are tone-deaf or have a poor sense of rhythm. NARRATORS 1 & 2 need a lot of rehearsal to fit the words to the music until they discover its flow. Advice on stage-fighting technique would not go amiss either if the actor playing ONE wants to live to see another day! After much perseverance you will find this piece quite powerful and it may prove particularly useful for teenage audiences.

'Mr G' does not stand on its own, however. It needs something to follow which moves us on to consider how this story applies to us. Jesus actually did this by asking the question 'What will the owner of the vineyard do to those tenants?' (Matt. 21: 40/Luke 20: 15.) His listeners answer in no uncertain terms and Jesus then moves them on to think about another picture representing God's purpose in sending his son (i.e. he quotes from Psalm 118: 22–3). It may be enough simply to pose two questions to leave in the audience's mind, e.g.: 'What do you think Mr G would do to Mr Right and his mob?' 'Do you think God has a right to punish us?' Either way it is essential to give this plenty of thought and prayer.

CHARACTERS: NARRATORS 1 AND 2 – Two singers, one ought to be a guitarist or able to play another suitable instrument.

Male (NARRATOR 1) and female (NAR-
rator 2) would be good. They become the crowd in the party and fight
scenes.

ONE – MR G, rent collector, and MR G'S
SON. Needs to have presence and a
sense of comic timing.

TWO – SHOP ASSISTANT and MR RIGHT,
super cool with a good sense of
rhythm.

THREE – SHOP ASSISTANT and PARTY-
GOER.

*The NARRATORS are situated half off the acting area on
extreme* SL *or* SR. ONE *(MR G) is seated on a chair* CS. *(He
could wear a waistcoat and a badge with a 'G' on it.)* TWO &
THREE *are either side (*SHOP ASSISTANTS*). Each mimes suitable actions during the opening sequence. The focus of
attention should be on* ONE *who is presumably in an office,
writing letters, answering the telephone, etc.*

NARRATORS: (*sing*) Bop shoo wahli wahli, bop
shoo wah!
Bop shoo wahli wahli, bop shoo wah!

NARRATOR 1: Let us introduce you to Mister G,
A man who runs his business so
successfully.

NARRATOR 2: He can sell you any food with ev'ry
kind of dressin'
Because the little shop he owns is a
high-class delicatessen.

NARRATORS: Bop shoo wahli wahli, bop shoo wah!

NARRATOR 2: The story that we tell you is a
tragedy,
For something's round the corner for
Mister G.

NARRATOR 1: 'Twas on a Monday morning the
telephone gave a loud ring.

NARRATORS: Now let's take a look and see what's
happening.
(*The following sequence proceeds in
rhythm without pauses unless stated.*
ONE *mimes a telephone,* TWO
*unpacking boxes and stacking
shelves, while* THREE *an electronic till
and handling money.*)

ONE: Dring, dring, dring dring.
Hello, good morning, Galsworthy
Smythe
Otherwise known as Mister G.

TWO: Peruvian pears

THREE: Eighty-six p.

ONE: All the best people buy from me.

TWO: African apricots

THREE: one pound and
four.

ONE: Mister G's the top class store.

THREE: Ninety-six pounds, thirty-four p.

ONE: What's that you say? Some news for
me? (TWO AND THREE *continue to
make comments and vocal sounds as*
ONE *builds his questioning to a quick,
small crescendo.*) Yes? Yes? Yes?
Oh! (*jumping up*) I've won! (*Pause.*
TWO & THREE *have stopped their noise
and gather round* ONE.)

TWO: Anything wrong?

THREE: Cup of tea?

TWO: We're here to help you,

TWO & THREE: Mister G.

ONE: I've won!

TWO: Won what?

THREE: Well, what can it be?

ONE: A competition!

TWO & THREE: Congratulations!
(*Slight pause.*)

THREE: Cup of tea?

TWO & THREE: Mister G?

ONE: A trip round the world.

TWO: How wonderful!

THREE: Marvellous!

TWO: Splendid!

THREE: How twee!

TWO & THREE: Congratulations! (*Slight pause.*)

THREE: Cup of tea?

TWO & THREE: Mister G?

ONE: (*worried*) Oh but I can't . . .

TWO & THREE: Oh but you can!

ONE: Oh but I mustn't . . .

TWO & THREE: Oh but you must!

ONE: Could I leave you to cope?

TWO & THREE: In us you can trust.

ONE: (*coming out of the rhythm*) Just think of it. Sunbathing on the top deck of an ocean liner . . . (*relishes the thought*) all around the world. (*Pause.*) All right, I'll go! Take the rest of the day off, both of you. (TWO & THREE *exeunt delighted.*) Hmm . . . but I must leave them in capable hands. (*Looks on his 'desk'.*) Let me see . . . Yellow pages! (*Flicks through the 'book'.*) Ah here we are . . . rent a toad, rent a tent, rent a tenant! What a marvellous idea. (*Picks up 'telephone' and pushes 'buttons'.*) Hello, good morning, could I rent a tenant? (*Freezes while chorus is sung, then mimes meeting people with appropriate reactions.*)

NARRATORS: Bop shoo wahli wahli, bop shoo wah!
Bop shoo wahli wahli, bop shoo wah!

NARRATOR 2: All kinds of people applied for the job

From flea-infested bums to intellectual snobs. (*After 'snobs',* THREE, *as* MR RIGHT, *enters opposite side of stage to* NARRATORS. *Super cool with sunglasses. Clicks on the off-beat after the end of each line.*)

NARRATOR 1: At last he found the man who matched each hope and aspiration,
The man he felt could easily cope with every situation.
(ONE *holds out hand to shake,* THREE *slaps it.*)

NARRATORS: Bop shoo wahli wahli, bop shoo wah! (*During this verse* THREE *holds out his hand,* ONE *slaps it on off-beat at the end of the first line. There is the mimed giving of a key which is quickly pocketed.* ONE *waves goodbye and* THREE *pushes him off the same side he has entered.*)

NARRATORS: Everything was peaches for Mister G.
Mister Right was put in charge and handed the key.
He went off on his holiday so totally unsuspecting,
Now let's take a look and see what's happening. (*Whispered.*) Yeah . . .

THREE: (*taking bass part. Clicks fingers. The accompaniment has stopped.* NARRATORS *put on identical sunglasses.*)
Bop shoo wahli wahli, bop shoo wah! (*He moves the chair* USC *so there is room for the dance.* TWO *enters wearing similar sunglasses clicking fingers singing melody. She passes* MR RIGHT *as though entering a door; they*

slap hands and bump hips.)

TWO & THREE: Bop shoo wahli wahli, bop shoo wah!
(NARRATORS *as* PARTYGOERS *follow*
TWO *and repeat sequence. One of
them sings 3rds, the other the top
part.*)

TWO, THREE
& NARRATOR: Bop shoo wahli wahli, bop shoo wah!

ALL: Bop shoo wahli wahli, bop shoo wah!
(*They continue to sing as they form a
line with the others. The dance should
give the impression of a seedy
nightclub. Develop basic, simple steps
in time with the rhythm, including
ideas such as drinking, each turning
back to audience and hugging self –
showing own hands on the back and
hips. After a sequence of eight beats
they turn back round, resume finger
clicking as backing for* THREE'*s verse.*)

ALL: Bop shoo wahli wahli, bop shoo wah!
Bop shoo wahli wahli, bop shoo wah!

THREE: (*sings melody*) Now we're living in a
world of luxury
With every kind of vice and wild
debauchery.
Mine's the den for dirty men's
perversity and sinning –
Exotic discotessen's where it's
happening! (*Whispered.*) Yeah!
(*Repeat dance.*)

ALL: Bop shoo wahli wahli, bop shoo wah!
Bop shoo wahli wahli, bop shoo . . .
(*They are interrupted by loud banging
provided by* ONE OS.) Argh! (*They all
freeze in a 'We've-been-caught-naked'
pose.*)

THREE: It's a raid! Quick! Bottles under the

table, and get your clothes on! (*They
panic. In a frenzy of activity they
mime dressing, hiding objects and end
up forming a polite gathering daintily
holding tea-cups, but they still have
their sunglasses on. Meanwhile* ONE
enters and arrives at 'door' as the RENT
COLLECTOR. *He wears a cloth cap, a
long raincoat and extremely thick
glasses. He is cross-eyed.*)

THREE: Right . . . stay cool (*mimes opening
the door.*)

ONE: Hello . . . are you Mr Right?

THREE: Right. Who are you?

ONE: I'm Mr G's financial adviser.
(*Crosses* THREE *to* CS.) And I've come
for the rent.

THREE: The what?

ONE: The rent.

THREE: The rent?

REST: The rent?

ONE: (*a little bemused*) The rent . . .

THREE: (*slightly threatening*) Well I'm sorry
my old mate but Mr G didn't
mention anything about rent. Did he
lads?

REST: (*extremely posh*) Nothing
whatsoever!

THREE: But seeing as how you've come all
this way, we'll have to see what we
can do. Ron! Pay the gentleman.

ONE: (*believing he is to be paid*) Oh, thank
you very much.
(NARRATOR 1 *steps forward, knees him
in the groin and breaks his arm over
his knee.* ONE *cries out in agony and is
thrown out by* NARRATOR 1 *and* THREE.
ONE *exits, hobbling. They dance and*

resume as before.)

ALL: Bop shoo wahli wahli, bop shoo wah!
Bop shoo wahli wahli, bop shoo . . .
(ONE *knocks again*.) Argh! (*They
freeze as before*.)

THREE: It's him again. Quick, bottles under
the table. And get your clothes on!
(*Frenzied activity as before but
quicker.* ONE *enters again, this time
with his arm in a sling*.) Right. Stay
cool. (*Mimes 'door'*.)

ONE: (*high-pitched*) Hello, it's me again.
(*Coughs. Low voice*.) Now look here
. . . Mr G said . . . (THREE *pulls him
across to* CS.)

THREE: We've already paid you once mate!
But seeing as you're so persistent
we'll pay you again. Ron! Give him
the next instalment. (NARRATOR 1
steps forward again.)

ONE: (*beginning to tremble*) Oh . . . no
. . . not now! Later, Ron . . .
(NARRATOR 1 *advances*.) Leave me
alone! (NARRATOR 1 *'nuts' him with
his head.* THREE *stamps on his foot*.
ONE *is thrown out. He exits clutching
head and attempting to clutch his foot
with his broken arm. Dancing
resumes again. This time it is a little
more disorderly and drunken*.)

ALL: Bop shoo wahli wahli, bop shoo wah!
Bop shoo wahli wa . . .
(ONE *knocks again. They attempt a
freeze*.) Hmm?

NARRATOR 2: Hic!

THREE: Not again! Right. (*Slurring slightly*.)
Clothes under the table. Bottles on.
(*They stare at him blankly*.) You

know what I mean. Do it! (*They
attempt it quickly.* ONE *enters limping,
having added a head bandage with
blood on.*) Right. Kay stool. (*He
opens the 'door'.* ONE *is about to
speak when* THREE *lands him a blow
on the chin.* ONE *falls to the ground.*)

ALL: Yeah! (*They sing and dance wildly.*
ONE *manages to get up and as he exits
he spits out 'teeth' (segments of Polo
mints). Meanwhile* NARRATORS *1 and 2
return to original positions, taking
sunglasses off.* THREE *slumps into
chair* USC *with* TWO *at his feet. The
noise subsides as* TWO *and* THREE
sleep.)

NARRATORS: Bop shoo wahli wahli, bop shoo wah!
Bop shoo wahli wahli, bop shoo wah!
Mister G's holiday was going just
fine.
When he got a message on the
telephone line.
The news he heard was terrible, it set
his heart a-racin'.

NARRATOR 1: The man he'd sent to c'llect the rent,
they'd gone and smashed his face in.

NARRATORS: Bop shoo wahli wahli, bop shoo wah!
Bop shoo wahli wahli, bop shoo wah!
(ONE *enters as* MR G'S SON *dressed in
well-to-do jacket. He mimes knocking
on the door and trying the handle.*)
He didn't want to go home, he was
having such fun.
He'd make them pay their debts to
him by sending his son.

NARRATOR 2: His son was filled with confidence
when he arrived that morning

NARRATORS: Now let's take a look and see what's

happening. (*Whispered.*) Yeah!

ONE: (*forces 'door' open*) Hello? (*Finds TWO and THREE who begin to stir.*) Looks like it was quite a party. (*Getting down to business.*) Right. Mr G sent me . . . he's my father.

THREE: (*who has stood up, approaches ONE tauntingly*) So you're Mr G's son eh? That's nice for you. (*Beckons TWO, NARRATORS 1 and 2, who put their sunglasses back on, to join him. THREE is more menacing.*) Mr G has sent his son now . . . (*They all surround ONE.*)

ONE: Are you Mr Right?

THREE: Yeah, so what?

ONE: I've come for the rent.

THREE: (*sneering*) He's come for the rent. (*Starts finger-click rhythm.*)

REST: (*joining in rhythm*) You've come for the rent? (*They all start to encircle ONE, keeping the rhythm. Gradually it becomes faster and more menacing.*)

THREE: It's money you want.

NARRATOR 2: There's nothing for you.

THREE: And now it's all mine.

TWO: So clear off out.

NARRATOR 1: And don't come back.
(*This is repeated two or three times, becoming more aggressive and accompanied by pushes and kicks. ONE drops to his knees, there is a frenzy of kicking and a cacophony of shouting as THREE draws ONE up, punches him in the stomach and pulls his head down sharply on to his knee. ONE collapses to floor and the noise and action suddenly cease. Silence.*)

> *Gradually we hear the nervous,*
> *shocked breathing of* TWO, THREE *and*
> NARRATORS *as they slowly back off.*
> *Each takes his sunglasses off. They*
> *are horrified by their actions.*
> NARRATORS *return slowly to their*
> *positions.* TWO *and* THREE *remain*
> *looking at the body.*)

NARRATORS: (*singing slowly and softly at first*)
Bop shoo wahli wahli, bop shoo wah!
Bop shoo wahli wahli, bop shoo wah!
Mister Right was now convinced the battle he'd won.
But Mister G was angry at the death of his son.
God has left you with your life and if you think you're winning,
Take a look again and see what's happening. (*Repeat*)
God has left you with your life and if you think you're winning,
Take a look again and see what's happening. (*Whispered.*) Yeah.

MR G

1. Bop shoo wahli wahli, bop shoo wah!
   Bop shoo wahli wahli, bop shoo wah!
   Let us introduce you to Mister G,
   A man who runs his business so successfully.
   He can sell you any food with ev'ry kind of dressin'
   Because the little shop he owns is a high-class delicatessen.
   Bop shoo wahli wahli, bop shoo wah!

The story that we tell you is a tragedy,
For something's round the corner for Mister G.
'Twas on a Monday morning the telephone gave a loud ring.
Now let's take a look and see what's happening. Yeah.

2. Bop shoo wahli wahli, bop shoo wah!
   Bop shoo wahli wahli, bop shoo wah!
   All kinds of people applied for the job
   From flea-infested bums to intellectual snobs.
   At last he found the man who matched each hope and aspiration,
   The man he felt could easily cope with every situation.
   Bop shoo wahli wahli, bop shoo wah!
   Everything was peaches for Mister G.
   Mister Right was put in charge and handed the key.
   He went off on his holiday so totally unsuspecting,
   Now let's take a look and see what's happening. Yeah.

   (Unaccompanied refrain)
   Ba ba ba boom, ba boom, ba boom, ba boom. (etc.)
   Bop shoo wahli wahli, bop shoo wah! (etc.)

3. Now we're living in a world of luxury,
   With every kind of vice and wild debauchery.
   Mine's the den for dirty men's perversity and sinning,
   Exotic discotessen's where it's happening. Yeah.

4. Bop shoo wahli wahli, bop shoo wah!
   Bop shoo wahli wahli, bop shoo wah!
   Mister G's holiday was going just fine,
   When he got a message on the telephone line.
   The news he heard was terrible, it set his heart a-racin',
   The man he'd sent to c'llect the rent they'd gone and smashed his face in.
   Bop shoo wahli wahli, bop shoo wah!
   He didn't want to go home he was having such fun.
   He'd make them pay their debts to him by sending his son.

His son was filled with confidence when he arrived that morning,
Now let's take a look and see what's happening. Yeah.

5. Bop shoo wahli wahli, bop shoo wah!
Bop shoo wahli wahli, bop shoo wah!
Mister Right was now convinced the battle he'd won.
But Mister G was angry at the death of his son.
God has left you with your life and if you think you're winning,
Take a look again and see what's happening. Yeah.

Music: Pip Hawthorn 1980

PEDESTALS

A musical sketch in the style of a melodrama. The four characters never speak but communicate with the audience with exaggerated facial expressions and mannerisms. They wear large, colourful items of costume and carry larger-than-life-sized props. The fifth character is dressed normally and sits at the piano throughout the piece, turning occasionally to provide the 'voices' of the other characters. This he does loudly and confidently but as if he is reading from a script. The music provides the main atmosphere and it is important that the movements and words are delivered taking into account the rhythm of it. The piece should move fairly briskly.

CHARACTERS: PIANIST — 'RICHES', 'FAME', 'BRAINS', 'JESUS', 'DEATH'.

> *Piano plays first few bars of 'If I were a rich man' from* 'Fiddler on the Roof'. *During this* RICHES *enters carrying a box, or chair, displaying a notice saying* 'Riches'. *He places his box either* SL *or* SR *leaving room for the other characters and* DEATH *on stage. The line of boxes and characters will eventually extend across the width of the stage at intervals of about a metre.* RICHES *stands on his box, smokes the obviously fake cigar and waves a huge bundle of banknotes in the air. As the*

> *music finishes he mouths the words:*

PIANIST: (*proudly*) I know what it is to be rich!
(*Piano plays first few bars of* 'There's no business like show business'. *During this* FAME *enters with box labelled* 'Fame'. *She places it next to* RICHES, *climbs on it and poses as if the audience were the press. She wears sunglasses, ostentatious hat and a cigarette in a holder. The music finishes and she mouths:*)

PIANIST: (*gushingly*) I know everyone worth knowing and they know me!
(*Piano plays a few bars of* 'Anything you can do I can do better'. BRAINS *enters looking extremely erudite with spectacles, a large pile of books and, possibly, a mortar-board. Her box is labelled* 'Brains'. *It is positioned next to* FAME *and she smiles short-sightedly over her glasses. She repeats the above technique.*)

PIANIST: (*with self-satisfaction*) I know everything there is to know!
(*Piano plays, very crisply,* 'Onward Christian soldiers' *as* JESUS *enters dressed brightly and carrying a large Bible. He marches briskly across the stage and places his box* 'Jesus' *to complete the line-up. He beams around the audience confidently as he stands on his box and mouths:*)

PIANIST: (*confidently*) I know God's Son!
(RICHES, FAME *and* BRAINS *mime laughing uproariously at* 'JESUS', *pointing and mocking.*)

PIANIST: (*loudly and slowly with absolutely no trace of emotion*)

Ha ha ha. Ha ha ha. Ha ha ha. Ha.
(*All four stop what they are doing
abruptly and turn to the* PIANIST *with a
disapproving stare. They cough.*)

RICHES ⎫
FAME   ⎪
BRAINS ⎬ : Ach – hemm!
'JESUS' ⎭

PIANIST: (*embarrassed*) Oh . . . sorry. (*He
laughs loudly and hysterically as the
others resume their movements.*)
(*Piano plays silent-movie style* 'Enter
the Baddie' *music.* DEATH *prowls in
menacingly, stalking round the stage
stroking an imaginary waxed
moustache.*

DEATH *is dressed all in black,
marked either* 'Death' *or with a skull
and crossbones. Music changes to a
death march. During this sequence*
DEATH *approaches each of the three
characters,* RICHES, BRAINS, FAME, *and
suitably timed to the music very
dramatically topples them from their
pedestals; each dies dramatically but
swiftly and lies still, spread-eagled on
the ground.* RICHES *lets his banknotes
flutter to the ground as he falls. As
each character falls, the* PIANIST *gives
a loud evil laugh. During this* 'JESUS'
*has been miming shouting warnings
to the others but they are all too
absorbed in their own world to notice*
DEATH *or him.* 'JESUS' *looks more and
more distressed at the events taking
place.* DEATH *finally attempts to push
him from his* 'JESUS' *box but he has
problems. The music becomes louder*

and faster as DEATH *kicks, shoves and generally becomes more agitated. Meanwhile* 'JESUS' *first looks worried, then prays hard, looks more worried, then prays fervently until his knees quake. Eventually he realises that* DEATH *has lost and hugs his Bible, smiles and looks confident as his box stands firm as a rock. He even mimes jeering and pointing at* DEATH. DEATH *ends up kicking the box frantically with silent-movie type acceleration. The music rises to a climax and stops abruptly as* DEATH *gives up and shouts at the audience.*)

DEATH: Curses! Foiled again!
(*He exits leaving* 'JESUS' *to give a thumbs-up sign heavenward and smiles as the piano plays the last two lines of* 'Onward Christian soldiers'.)

INTRODUCING THAT JAUNTING JACKANAPES . . . JONAH!

A piece which relies heavily on rhythm and comedy atmosphere to tell a well-known story with a new emphasis. The setting is an Edwardian music hall. The three characters (two performers and a pianist) wear striped blazers, sport handlebar moustaches and speak with pronounced 'auxford ecksense'. Throughout the piece the pace is set by the pianist who vamps on the piano at a bouncy tempo. The two performers walk smartly on the spot in time to the music and speak the words rhythmically, loudly and in a proclamatory fashion – a little like the chairman in the BBC's 'Good Old Days'. The words are almost like a spoken song, delivered in verses grouped in pairs, with a short refrain between each pair. This gives a natural punctuation to the delivery and the accompanying actions form a kind of comic dance. We have given suggested actions but you will probably find it easier to learn the song first and then invent movements of your own to fit with your own patterns of speech.

You will inevitably find it difficult to keep the speed of this piece under control. If you are not careful you end up going so fast that the actors cannot keep up, never mind the audience! But it is great fun to perform and to watch, and even funnier to rehearse.

WARNING Do not even attempt this sketch if you have little, or no sense of rhythm.

All suggested actions appear in brackets after the relevant lines, but they are intended to be performed as the lines are delivered.

CHARACTERS: PIANIST, PERFORMER A, PERFORMER B.

> *Enter* PIANIST *with great
> self-importance. He takes his seat at
> the piano. Immediately the music
> begins,* A, *who acts as narrator, enters*
> SL *and walks in time to the music* DSC.
> A *and* B *walk on the spot throughout.*

A: Here's Jonah, son of Amittai
(*He indicates* SR.)
The one of whom we sing
(*Enter* B SR. *He walks* DSC *to* A.)
A goodly man of God was he
But he liked to do his own thing.

He planned his life, two kids, one
wife
(B *counts children, puts arm round*
'wife'.)
A semi on the beach
(B *indicates house*.)
And in the local synagogue
Each sabbath he would preach.
(B 'preaches'.)

A&B: (*singing*) But God said
Start all over again!
(*They perform a short routine of steps
during the few bars between chorus
and the next verse. They end up* DSC.)

A: God said 'You go to Nineveh
(*He points to* B *who looks suitably
worried*.)
And tell them what I say.
Their wickedness has gone too far
And now the price they'll pay.'

But Jonah said

B: I'll not go there

Although I really oughta.
(*Folds arms with defiant expression.*)

A: So he packed his suitcase, paid his fare
(B *mimes suitable actions.*)
And sailed across the water.
(*Both indicate waves.*)

PIANIST: (*interrupting sarcastically*)
In the opposite direction of course!

A&B: (*as before*) But God said

PIANIST: You're going the wrong way!

A: But Jonah wasn't listening
(B *covers ears and shuts eyes.* A *does routine as before.* B *is left, realises, but can't catch up. Both return* DSC.)

A: Jonah he was happy
He thought he'd got away.
(B *looking pleased with himself.*)
Till God sent storms, the wind, the waves,
And the ship began to sway.
(*Both rock and lurch.*)

B: The sailors said I was to blame
They chucked me in the sea.

A: Splosh!

B: A great big fish came swimming by
And gobbled me up for tea.
(A *mimes events.*)

PIANIST: (*stopping the music, thereby catching* A *and* B *by surprise*)
I say, I say, I say!

A&B: (*slightly annoyed*) What do you say?

PIANIST: Heard the one about Jonah?

A&B: No?

PIANIST: Got swallowed up by a great big fish
– had a whale of a time! (A *and* B *groan loudly. Music and routine resume.*)

A: For three long days he sat inside
That great big fish's tum.
(B *looks around, holds nose, etc.*)
And there he had the time to think
Of all that he had done.

He said to God

B: You've made your point
I'm ready to do your will.
I promise to go to Nineveh.
Just make this fish feel ill.

PIANIST: (*with great relish*) Spewed him up it
did . . . all over the beach!

A&B: (*shocked*) Really!
(*Singing.*) And God said

PIANIST: All right, I'll let you . . .

A&B: Start all over again!
(*Routine to* DSC.)

A: So off he went to Nineveh
To preach to the people there
(B *using audience as people to preach
to.*)

B: Walk around in sackcloth
Put ashes in your hair
You've forty days to do it in
Listen what God has said –
He says you must repent your sins
Or else you'll all be dead!
(A *reacts to* B*'s preaching and
gradually sinks to the floor with
exaggerated repentance and guilt.
Both are kneeling by the end. During
the following they rise gradually as
they also take each phrase a pitch
higher than the last to give a sense of
building excitement.*)

A&B: And they listened . . .
And they lived . . .

And God said . . .
I'll let you . . .
(*They are standing.*)
Start all over again!
(*On the concluding two beats of the
music* A&B *perform suitable
proclamatory poses.*)

With special thanks to Brian Radcliffe,
Steve Summers and Robert Rogers.

INTRODUCING THAT JAUNTING
JACKANAPES . . . JONAH!

1. Here's Jonah, son of Amittai
   The one of whom we sing
   A goodly man of God was he
   But he liked to do his own thing.
   He planned his life, two kids, one wife
   A semi on the beach
   And in the local synagogue
   Each sabbath he would preach.
   But God said
   Start all over again!

2. God said 'You go to Nineveh
   And tell them what I say.
   Their wickedness has gone too far
   And now the price they'll pay.'
   But Jonah said 'I'll not go there
   Although I really oughta.'
   So he packed his suitcase, paid his fare
   And sailed across the water.
   (In the opposite direction of course!)
   But God said
   (You're going the wrong way!)

3. Jonah he was happy
   He thought he'd got away.
   Till God sent storms, the wind, the waves,
   And the ship began to sway.
   'The sailors said I was to blame
   They chucked me in the sea (Splosh!)
   A great big fish came swimming by
   And gobbled me up for tea.'

4. For three long days he sat inside
   That great big fish's tum.
   And there he had the time to think
   Of all that he had done.
   He said to God 'You've made your point
   I'm ready to do your will.
   I promise to go to Nineveh
   Just make this fish feel ill.'
   (Spewed him up it did . . . all over the beach!) (Really!)
   And God said (All right I'll let you)
   'Start all over again!'

5. So off he went to Nineveh
   To preach to the people there.
   Walk around in sackcloth
   Put ashes in your hair
   You've forty days to do it in
   Listen to what God has said
   He says you must repent of your sins
   Or else you'll all be dead!
   And they listened . . .
   And they lived . . .
   And God said . . .
   'I'll let you . . .
   Start all over again!'

Music: Nigel Styles 1980

L.H. to be played an
octave lower throughout.

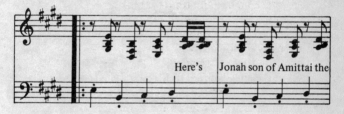

Here's Jonah son of Amittai the

one of whom we sing. A goodly man of God was he but he

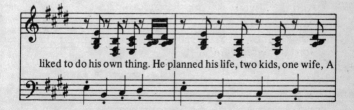

liked to do his own thing. He planned his life, two kids, one wife, A

SECTION 3 – FAST, FURIOUS AND THOUGHTFUL

i Shorter pieces

PLANE SAILING

Originally written for a Christian audience, this short play about Jonah can have a much wider appeal. Do not attempt this until you have used the workshop ideas on p. 17). You will also discover the crucial need to play some trust games: the type where individuals take it in turn to be cradled and caught by other group members. (See p. 25 in *Using the Bible in Drama* by the authors or books such as *Theatre Games* by Clive Barker.) The person playing ONE (Jonah) must be able to trust the other group members implicitly, in fact, everyone must concentrate one hundred per cent in order to make the particular stunt in this piece work. (It should be rehearsed *dozens* of times.)

The performance should give the audience the impression that they are watching a type of cartoon. This doesn't mean that the actors are simply being silly, but that they are watching a caricature, an exaggeration which helps to communicate Jonah's foolhardy attitudes and, hopefully, ours too. 'Plane Sailing' should proceed at a brisk, almost breathless, pace at first. Although apparently copious at first sight the stage directions are vital to its success; in fact the piece is nowhere near as long as it appears on the first read through.

Because every member needs good rhythmic timing, not

every group will find they are confident to take this on. Quite right too – it's not plain sailing.

CHARACTERS: ONE – Becomes JONAH. A thick Brummy accent, in fact a thick Brummy. He is likeable and vulnerable.

TWO – Male. Needs to be physically quite strong.

THREE – Male. Becomes God, whose voice should be very friendly and firm.

FOUR – Female.

FIVE – Male.

SIX – Female. Becomes Jonah's wife. A longsuffering and understanding Brummy wife, most of the time . . .

There is a stepladder USC upon which hangs a large, gold acoustic megaphone and a pilot's type cap. A chair is DSR with an item of suitable costume for JONAH. All actors enter and stand with backs to audience in a line across the stage slightly DS of the ladder. Actor TWO (from the SL end) turns and walks to CS whistling a suitable tune, in the manner of a stereotype policeman.

TWO: Evenin' all. Nineveh: a city of opportunity.

ONE: (*who has turned from SR end of line, as a criminal*) And here's my opportunity! (*He mimes hitting TWO on the head and stealing from his pocket.*) Bop!

TWO: Ouch! Stop thief! (ONE *runs, cartoon style round the edge of the acting area to US. TWO pursues in similar style. ONE dodges through the stepladder USC and runs on the spot SL of ladder. TWO stays SR of ladder also running on the spot. Both caricature running, it is not realistic. At the same time as this*

THREE, FOUR *and* FIVE *have formed a
police car –* ONE *kneels and steers, the
other two stand over him creating the
impression of flashing lights. They all
jog and sway according to the
'cornering'.*)

THREE
FOUR } : Bee baa! Bee baa! Bee baa!
FIVE

TWO: Stop thief!

ONE: Ya ha haa!

TWO: Stop thief!

ONE: Ya ha haa! (*They move off still
running.* ONE *passes in front of the
police car to end* SR. TWO *passes under
ladder ending* SL. *It should be timed
so that the police car screeches to a
halt just as* ONE *passes in front of it.*)

THREE
FOUR } : Bee baa! Bee baa! (*They all provide a
screech of brakes, pitch forward then
FIVE back together.* ONE *and* TWO *also stop.
There is a momentary stillness.*)

THREE: (*to audience*) Nineveh: where there's
always a party.

FOUR: And most people are party to
anything! (*There is a general whoop
of merriment.* THREE *and* FOUR *dance
together.* SIX *mimes suitable actions
while singing* 'The Stripper'. *Others
mime general party goings-on with
accompanying vocal sound effects.*
SIX *contrives an exit* SL. TWO *blows a
whistle. They all freeze, shocked.*)

TWO: It's a raid!

ALL: Arrgh! (*Momentary stillness.*)

FIVE: (*to audience*) Nineveh: where the
kids rule . . .

ALL: Okay? (*They all taunt and

*cock-a-snook at imaginary figures
off.*) Naa naa na naa naa! (*They blow
a raspberry to the audience in unison.
Momentary stillness.*)

TWO: (*speaking to audience and moving
DSL*) Nineveh: where they play
Happy Families . . .

ONE: But nobody ever wins.
(*They all form a line across DS area.
The following comments pass from
person to person along the line
with suitable gestures and
characterisations. A regular rhythm is
kept.*)

TWO: Who's pinched me teeth?

THREE: (*to TWO*) Shut your mouth, Grandad.

FIVE: (*to THREE*) You've been on the booze
again.

ONE: (*to FIVE*) I've wet me pants.

FOUR: (*to anyone, as a baby*) Waah! Waah!
Waah! Waah! (*They all repeat
respective line simultaneously
maintaining the rhythm, except FOUR
who cries only twice*)

TWO: (*to THREE*) Shut your face!

THREE: (*to FIVE*) Shut your face!

FIVE: (*to ONE*) Shut your face!

ONE: (*to FOUR*) Shut your face!

ONE
TWO   ⎫
THREE ⎬ : (*mime hitting respective victim*)
FIVE   ⎭   Whack!

FOUR: Waaah! (*All pause momentarily.
During the following ONE moves to
chair, puts on jumper and sits
watching the action, which we realise
has been on the television. He is
open-mouthed and suitably stunned.*

*The remaining four perform an
appropriate short song and dance to
the following.*)

TWO
THREE
FOUR   } : Nineveh! Nineveh!
FIVE

TWO: Amazing!
THREE: Sparkling!
FIVE: Dazzling!
FOUR: Corrupting!

TWO
THREE
FOUR   } : Nineveh! Nineveh needs you! (*They
FIVE   point to the audience but then
            change the direction to* ONE *who has
            become* JONAH.)

THREE: Yes friends, Nineveh needs you!
(ONE *leans forward switching off the
'television'.* TWO, FIVE *and* FOUR
exeunt, THREE *climbs the stepladder
and stands at the top with the
megaphone to his lips, becoming* GOD.
Enter SIX *as* JONAH'S WIFE *carrying
(mimed) cups of tea.*)

SIX: Oh, Jonah, you switched the telly
off.

ONE: Yeah I know. Mary Whitehouse
ought to do something about places
like that.

SIX: Somebody certainly ought to do
something about places like that. I
was reading in the newspaper only
the other day that they want people
to go and work in Nineveh.

ONE: Oh really? (*Drinks tea.*)

THREE: Yes Jonah, that's exactly why I want
you to go there.

ONE: (*with a slight splutter*) Pardon?

SIX: I said . . . I was reading in the

newspaper the other day they want
people to go and work in Nineveh.

THREE: The people of Nineveh have turned
against me. They have to say sorry.

ONE: Sorry?

SIX: (*a little exasperated*) I said . . . they
want people to work in Nineveh.

THREE: Tell them they have forty days to
repent otherwise I'll destroy them.
(ONE *is standing looking quizzically
upwards*.) It all depends on you
Jonah.

ONE: (*amazed*) You what?

SIX: (*screaming*) People to work . . . in
Nineveh!

ONE: (*to* SIX) Sorry dear, did you say
something?

SIX: Flippin' heck you never listen to
anything I say, do you?

ONE: Hey. You've got a point there love.
Pack us a suitcase will you? I've
decided to go on a long journey. (*He
mimes putting a coat on.*)

SIX: (*to* AUDIENCE) I bet he's going to that
wicked city. (*Fetching a 'suitcase'.*)
What a hero, what a man of God.
(*Hands him 'case'.*) There you are,
love.

ONE: Ta, love. (*He picks up 'case' and
holds out cheek for a kiss.* SIX *obliges
and begins waving as he starts to exit.*)

SIX: Send us a postcard from Nineveh,
Jonah.

ONE: (*stopping in his tracks*) Nineveh? I'd
rather go to Birmingham than
Nineveh. I'm off to Costa del Tarshish.

SIX: (*to audience*) I thought he was going
to Nineveh . . . (*She exits as* THREE

*sits down, puts megaphone back and
dons cap, becoming Tannoy voice
complete with vibrato nasal effects.
Meanwhile* ONE *walks across* DS, USL,
back to CS *by which time he literally
bumps into* TWO, FOUR *and* FIVE.)

THREE: Bing bong! Will passengers for flight
one, zero, five please go to the
departure lounge. Thank you.
(TWO, FOUR *and* FIVE *have entered
providing a tide of travellers bumping
into one another and against which*
ONE *has to struggle to the other side of
the stage. They mime pushing
trolleys, carrying heavy luggage, etc.
We hear ad lib. comments from* ONE
above the hubbub.)

TWO		Grumble, grumble,
FOUR	: (*unison*)	grumble, etc.
FIVE		Push, push, push, push, etc.
		Moan, moan, moan, moan, etc.

(*During the following
announcement* TWO, FOUR *and* FIVE
form a line across DS *about 1.5
metres apart, each in applicable pose
plus huge smiles. Meanwhile* ONE *is
left dizzy and bemused.*)

THREE: Bing bong! Will passengers for Costa
del Tarshish please check in now.
(ONE *staggers to* FIVE. *The following
rhythm is accompanied by suitable
actions.*)

FIVE: Hello sir, ticket?

ONE: Costa del Tarshish.

FIVE: Scribble, scribble, rip. There you
are, sir.

ONE: Thank you.

FIVE: Thank you, sir. (*Resumes pose.* ONE *moves to* FOUR.)

FOUR: Hello sir, luggage?

ONE: Costa del Tarshish.

FOUR: Pick, lick, stick. There you are, sir.

ONE: Thank you.

FOUR: Thank you, sir. (*Resumes pose.* ONE *moves to* TWO.)

TWO: Hello sir, passport?

ONE: Costa del Tarshish.

TWO: Squelch, stamp, stamp. (*About to hand 'passport' back, changes mind.*) Stamp, stamp, stamp, stamp, stamp! (*With cheesy grin.*) There you are, sir!

ONE: (*doubtfully*) Thank you.

TWO: Thank you, sir. (*He resumes pose.* ONE *moves past him on his way.*)

TWO
FOUR }: (*to audience*) I thought he was going to Nineveh.
FIVE

ONE: (*turning back*) Pardon?

TWO
FOUR }: (*Turning heads to* ONE) Nothing! (*They turn back to audience, smiling.* ONE *shrugs.*)
FIVE

THREE: Bing bong! Will passengers for Costa del Tarshish please go to gate five. Thank you.
(TWO, FOUR *and* FIVE *have moved* US *by the ladder.* FOUR *and* FIVE *form 'wings' either side of the ladder with their heads bowed.* TWO *forms a 'propellor' with arms at the foot of the ladder* CS.)

ONE: So . . . I make my way to gate five to get on me plane. Hee hee! (*He starts to cross the stage but is stopped.*)

THREE: (*As tannoy*) Oi, you!

ONE: (*looking up*) Who, me?

THREE: Yes, you! I thought you were going to Nineveh?

ONE: No I'm flippin' well not! (*He starts the 'propellor' with a sharp pull. The plane throbs into life with* TWO *providing loud vocal effects of a rasping faltering bi-plane ticking over.* ONE *climbs the ladder.* THREE *forms the tail of the plane with head bowed, having taken off his hat. The plane revs then 'takes off'. This is achieved by all raising heads and adding roars rather than the existing raspberry sound. The engine swells as everybody surges up and back. Once airborne,* THREE, FOUR *and* FIVE *hum,* TWO *continues engine noise.*) So here I am full-pelt for Costa del Tarshish without any sign of God anywhere. Hee hee! But at thirty thousand feet we hit a storm. (*Plane noise ceases.* TWO, THREE, FOUR *and* FIVE *all clap loudly once.*) And the storm hits back!

ALL: Crash! Bang! Wallop! (*Plane formation is broken. The actors provide thunder, lightning and wind noises as they move to* TWO *either side of the ladder, crouching. They tip the ladder from side to side slowly.* ONE *leans the opposite way as it does so.*)

ONE: The plane lurches and begins to rock and roll all over the sky! The passengers begin to panic. They bring out their rabbit's feet, their Saint Christophers and their American Express cards! So I make

my way back and hide in the toilet.
(*He has moved up the ladder and
mimes shutting a door. The storm
noise diminishes, the ladder is only
being shaken slightly*) But a couple of
minutes later they drag me out again!

FOUR: (*Bobbing up. Australian*) Come out
of there, sport.

FIVE: (*Bobbing up. Scottish*) Stop hiding
away, Jimmy. (*They both bob down.*)

THREE: (*Bobbing up. American*) Come out
of the john, John.

TWO: (*Bobbing up. French*) It's all his
fault. (*They both bob down.*)

FOUR ⎫
FIVE ⎭ : (*Bobbing up*) He's running away
from God! (*They bob down again.
Storm noise resumes.*)

ONE: You're right, I *am* running away
from God! But I've thought of a way
to stop the storm. I'm going to jump
out of the plane.

TWO ⎫
THREE ⎪
FOUR ⎬ : (*all bobbing up*) Don't do it! (*All go
FIVE ⎭   back down.*)

ONE: It's no good. It's the only way you're
going to be saved. So I makes me
way to the rear door and open it. (*He
mimes opening a stiff hatch with a
heave. As soon as he does so the
storm ceases,* TWO, THREE, FOUR *and
FIVE move* DSC *crouching low, heads
covered with arms, swaying. They
also provide whooshing and
wind-whistling effects.*) Down below
I can see all the clouds whirling
around. Oh well, here goes . . .
Geronimo!

(*He dives from the top of the ladder as high as he can and is caught by the other actors who have stood up to catch him. For maximum effect split-second timing is essential. They lurch him up and down a couple of times with a few 'Arghs!' from* ONE. *The wind noise is sustained throughout. He is then transferred on to the back of* TWO, *who bends over underneath him, hands on knees so that his back forms a table.* TWO's *head is bowed, he continues wind effects throughout the following. Once* ONE *is in place, tummy downwards on* TWO, *facing the audience,* FOUR *and* FIVE *become birds. They flap their way* OS *by crossing over in front of* ONE *and* TWO, *thus providing cover for any necessary adjustment or repositioning which they need. The birds give a few raucous caws. They exeunt.* THREE *has climbed the ladder during this and is standing at the top with megaphone as God.* ONE *is spreadeagled as though free-falling.*)

Ooh! I'm going to be speared to death on the Pyrenees! Goodbye cruel world! (TWO *continues to give* ONE *floating movement by bending knees and swaying.*)

THREE: Hello, Jonah, nice of you to drop by.

ONE: Oh . . . Hello, God. Here . . . what's going on? What's happening?

THREE: Oh, nothing much. You've been falling through the air for three days that's all.

ONE: Oh great! A miracle, fantastic! Praise the Lord!

THREE: Thank you very much.

ONE: Look, Lord. I'm sorry I disobeyed you, really I am.

THREE: You've learnt your lesson then have you?

ONE: Yeah! I'll do anything you tell me to.

THREE: Even Nineveh?

ONE: Yeah . . . I'll even go to Nineveh!

THREE: Good. Well don't worry. I'll be with you all the time. (TWO *slowly turns so that they are both facing the ladder. Enter* FIVE SR.)

FIVE: So Jonah came down to earth with a bump. (TWO *ejects* ONE DS. ONE *crumples in a heap*.) Right in the middle of Nineveh.

ONE: (*getting up, checking his body*) And not a bone broken! Hee hee! (*He exits* SR. THREE *descends ladder and hangs megaphone on it.* TWO *moves ladder to* SL *and sits halfway up becoming a grossly fat, ugly barman.* THREE *joins him as a drunk who keeps trying to speak but rarely manages it. He holds a 'drink'.*)

FIVE: (*as a drunken Scot*) Knock knock!

TWO: I'm coming.

FIVE: Knock knock!

TWO: Who's there?

FIVE: Esme.

TWO: Esme who?

FIVE: Ets me, I want a drink! (*All three laugh and* FIVE *joins* THREE *at the foot of the ladder*.)

TWO: I haven't seen you round here lately.

FIVE: No. I've had a bad attack of yaws.

THREE: (*finally managing it*) What's yaws?

FIVE: Whisky! Make it a pint! (*They all laugh.*)

TWO: (*mimes pulling a pint*) Gush. Gush. (*Hands it to* FIVE.) There you go. (*Takes his own 'glass'.*)

TWO ⎫
THREE ⎬ : Cheers! (*They mime chinking glasses.*) Chink! (*They drink.*)
FIVE ⎭ Glug, glug, glug, glug, glug . . . (*They continue their activities silently.*)

ONE: (*having entered* DSR *holding a sheaf of papers*) Oh well, now I'm here I s'pose I'd better get on with writing my sermon. Now let me see . . . how can I start? Ah, I know. (*He 'writes'.*) Good people of Nineveh . . . (*He looks across to the others and catches a particularly nasty combination of grimaces. Scared, he writes again.*) *Bad* people of Nineveh . . . my text for today is the Old Testament (*looks at audience*) minus the book of Jonah 'cos it's not quite finished yet. Hee, hee! Let's give it a try. (*Clears throat and turns to them with an exhorting hand held high.*) Bad people of Nineveh . . . (FOUR *enters* USR *of* ONE, *waving to the other three. They wave back.*)

TWO ⎫
THREE ⎬ : Hello!
FIVE ⎭

(ONE *thinks they are waving back to him and chickens out. He turns back to his sermon.* FOUR *moves to the others* SL. *She can't walk in a straight line.*)

FOUR: (*slurring*) Hello, darlings, I've got a
job in painting and decorating . . .

FIVE: Oh, what's that?

FOUR: I'm a stripper! (*All four laugh in
exaggerated style.*)

TWO: Here, have a drink.

TWO ⎱
THREE ⎰ : Cheers! (*as before*) Chink! Glug,
FOUR   glug, glug, glug, glug . . . (*They
FIVE ⎰ continue activities silently again.*)

ONE: (*writing*) . . . eternal judgment.
Right. (*He looks at them.*) Oh dear,
they look worse than the people on
the telly. How did those preachers do
it in the old days? I remember! (*He
stands on a chair and assumes an
awesome authority. He is the
mightiest Welsh preacher of all time.
To audience.*) When the great day of
judgment comes you will stand
condemned before the Lord. (*The
others, who cannot hear him,
coincidentally laugh in silence. ONE is
getting carried away.*) And the
heavens will open and the fire and
the brimstone and the burning hot
sulphur will be heaped upon your
heads! (*He gets down and becomes
JONAH again.*) Yeah, something like
that I think.

FOUR: And *he* said to me . . . No I won't sit
on the floor, because . . . it's beneath
me! (*They all laugh.*)

TWO ⎱
THREE ⎰ : Cheers! Chink! Glug, glug, glug,
FOUR   glug, glug . . .
FIVE ⎰

ONE: (*writing*) The end. There . . . I think

forty-five points ought to do it. Okay,
God, here I go, your servant, off to
face the music. (*The rest start singing
and laughing, etc. He moves to them
and attempts to start reading his
sermon. It has no effect. He coughs.*)
Excuse me . . . (*They carry on. He
speaks louder.*) Excuse me . . . (*They
still haven't heard him.*) Excuse me!
(*Their noise ceases immediately. They
look simultaneously at the audience,
then at him.* ONE *squirms and gives a
nervous laugh. Silence. They are
staring angrily at him. He tries to
break the ice.*) Hello everybody . . .
(*They leer at him.*) er . . . um . . .
I've got a burden on my heart which I
feel led to share with you.
(*They move threateningly into a
group.*)

TWO ⎫
THREE ⎬ : Yes?
FOUR ⎪
FIVE ⎭

ONE: It's a message actually . . . from
God.

TWO ⎫
THREE ⎬ : (*as they take one step towards him*)
FOUR ⎪ Yes?
FIVE ⎭

ONE: The trouble is . . . I don't think
you're going to like it very much . . .

TWO ⎫
THREE ⎬ : (*another step, more menace*) Yes?
FOUR ⎪
FIVE ⎭

ONE: (*floundering, gibbering and backing
towards the chair*) Erm . . . You see

I've got this sermon to preach at you
. . . Er! *For* you!

TWO ⎫
THREE ⎬ : *(another step which forces* ONE *on to*
FOUR ⎪ *the chair)* Yes? (ONE *sifts desperately*
FIVE ⎭ *through his notes. The others have*
turned very nasty.) Yes?

ONE: *(screws up his notes and throws them*
over his shoulder. He closes his eyes
and rattles off his speech. On the
word 'Repent' *the other four sink*
immediately to their knees with a wail.
They bow down, heads to the floor.)
People of Nineveh you must repent
and turn from your wicked ways,
otherwise you will bring upon
yourselves God's condemnation and
fire and brimstone and burning hot
sulphur . . . *(realises that something*
is wrong) . . . will be heaped upon
your heads . . . er . . . what are you
doing down there?

FIVE: *(kneeling up suddenly)* We're
repenting.

FOUR: *(kneeling up suddenly)* We're turning
back to God.

THREE: *(same again)* We're saying sorry.

TWO: *(following suit)* We want to change.
(They all suddenly return to their
bowed-down positions.)

ONE: *(amazed)* Honestly?

TWO ⎫
THREE ⎬ : *(kneeling up suddenly)* Honestly!
FOUR ⎪ *(They freeze.)*
FIVE ⎭

ONE: *(to audience)* And they did want to
change. And do you know
something? God forgave them.
Yeah, just like that. No fire. No

brimstone. No nothing. Just heaps and heaps of forgiveness. It was really boring. (*An idea strikes him.*) Hey! (*He goes to the megaphone and picks it up.*) What a twit I am. I should have listened to God in the first place. It just goes to show what happens when you obey him, don't it? Here . . . (*He moves DSC and speaks through the megaphone.*) What has God asked you to do recently?

Note: This last question could be adjusted slightly to suit the event.

ACTION REPLAY

Sometimes it is good to complement a programme of lively, 'action-packed' sketches with a more low-key episode. Although the situation here is a totally unrealistic one, the two characters are only slightly larger than life, and the general atmosphere of tension which should prevail, must be communicated by subtle movements of uneasiness rather than melodramatic tremblings and groans.

'Action Replay' could also be used alongside, or as part of, a talk or address – as long as the speaker is sensitive to the atmosphere necessary to make it 'work'.

CHARACTERS: A ⎫ – Two rough and ready lads who
              B ⎭   normally cope with life easily, but here they are hopelessly out of their depth.

Both stand US *side by side with backs to the audience. There are two chairs* DS *about twelve feet apart.* A *turns and walks to a chair* SL *looking around in wonder and awe with a suggestion of fear.* B *follows slightly after. He is apparently checking to see if his head is still firmly attached to his body. Without seeing each other they sit. They are cold and uneasy.* A *notices* B. *He is about to speak, changes his mind then tries again.*

A: Hello! (*Smiles.*)
B: (*taken by surprise, turns quickly*)
   Oh . . . hello . . . (*Goes back to looking around nervously. Pause.*)
A: You dead then?

B: (*looks at* A, *encouraged*) Yeah!

A: Me too!

B: Great! (*They move their chairs together* SC, *both reassured*.) It's a ropey old place this, ain't it?

A: Yeah, like an old warehouse.

B: Freezing cold.

A: Horrible! (*Pause*.) Well, what happens now?

B: Dunno, I've just got here. (*Pause*.) Hey! How did you die then?

A: Me?

B: Yeah.

A: Well, electrician, right? I was fitting this cooker into some old girl's house and there was this wire hanging out of the wall. I grabs hold of it, don't I? Next thing I know: flash, bang, wallop, here I am.

B: Shocking.

A: Yeah. (*Pause*.) What about you then?

B: Well (*stands and mimes driving a car*) I was tonning down the motorway in me sports car, when suddenly, this juggernaut coming the other way must have gone out of control and burst across the central reservation. Before I knew where I was, I was under the back wheels, and there's me head rolling off down the centre lane. (*Sits*.)

A: Eurgh!

B: (*moving head from side to side*) Can't understand it really.

A: Looks all right now.

B: Can't see the join can you? (*Pause*.)

A: 'Ere, bet you thought you'd have to

carry that under your arm now, eh?
(*He laughs.* B *is not amused.*)

B: Eh?

A: (*laugh fizzles out*) Nothing . . .
(*Pause.*) What do you suppose
they're gonna do with us then? (*Both
turn sharply and look* USC *about ten
feet up.*)

B: (*as he turns*) What's that?

A: It's a light, flashing.

B: What do you think it means?

A: Dunno, some sort of signal I s'pose.

B: Signal for what?

A: For us? I mean, we're the only
people here.

B: Yeah.

A: Better go and see what they want
then. After you.

B: Cheers . . . (*He rises and nervously
walks* US. *He turns back.*) Are you
coming then . . . (A *has already got to
his feet.* B *smiles nervously. They both
move* US *and freeze in their original
positions. Hold for five seconds.* A
*turns round slowly, shocked, walks
slowly back to chair and sits.* B *does
the same. They are stunned.*)

A: You just been judged then?

B: Yeah . . . I think that's what he
called it.

A: Rough, weren't it?

B: Rough!

A: What I want to know is where they
get all their information from!

B: Right – all that film.

A: Everything I'd ever done in my life,
in glorious technicolour.

B: Yeah! Do you know they even

showed when I was twelve and we
used to pump up frogs with bicycle
pumps.

A: Yeah? (*Can't believe it.*) And every
word I've ever said . . . the swear
words, the lot . . . on tape!

B: Reel to reel.

A: Stereo. (*Pause.*)

B: And the thoughts, that's the worse
thing. They showed me all I'd ever
thought about anything. All my
opinions, all my decisions even my
prayers . .

A: Yer wot?

B: (*slightly embarrassed*) Prayers.

A: (*scornfully*) Used to pray did you?

B: (*defensive*) Well . . . yeah . . .
Christian, ain't I?

A: (*not interested*) Oh yeah?

B: (*realising*) Why . . . ain't you then?

A: Naaa! Used to think that was a load
of rubbish, (*looks round*) beginning
to wonder now though . . . still, it
hasn't got you very far has it? I mean,
you're in the same boat as I am . . .
being judged and all that (*laughs*)
. . . can't deny that. (*Both startled
again. They turn* USC.)

B: There it is again!

A: What do you s'pose they want this
time?

B: I don't know, do I?

A: Look, you go this time.

B: (*indignant*) Me?

A: Yeah, I had enough the first time!
Besides, you're s'posed to know
them better than I do. (*Smiles
sarcastically.* B *rises, shrugs and*

turns, worried, to US. *He walks to original position and freezes.* A *rises, paces a little way. Tries to shrug it off.* A *worrying thought strikes him.*) I wonder what they're gonna do with all those films, all those tapes?

B: (*has turned round, miming holding a stack of film and tape reels*) I've got them here.

A: (*turning, surprised*) What all of them?

B: Yeah. All of them.

A: Mine as well?

B: (*putting them on his chair*) Yours as well.

A: Well . . . (*reading a 'label'*) what have we got to do with them?

B: He said (*picks up 'top half' and gives them to* A) you've got to take yours through that door (*indicates imaginary door* SL) and down the stairs – only watch out as you get to the bottom as it gets a bit hot. (*Picks up his own films.*)

A: Oh . . . right. What you gotta do with yours?

B: Well . . . (*tentatively*) . . . I've got to throw mine away.

A: (*harshly*) Throw 'em away?

B: That's what he said . . . throw them away. (*Laughs, embarrassed.*)

A: Oh . . . right. (*Goes to walk away* SL.) Hang on (*turning back*) if you can throw yours away, why can't I throw mine away? I'm not taking these down there with me, it's incriminating evidence. I'm going to get rid of them. You watch. (*During the following he makes repeated attempts to throw them away.*) They won't go . . . they're stuck to my hands . . . d'you hear . . . they won't go! (*Pause.*) Right. (*Laughs nervously but is truly worried.*) See you then . . . (B *attempts to speak but nothing comes out.* A *turns and walks towards* SL, *stoops as if to go down a flight of stairs, and freezes.* B *watches him leave, laughs uncertainly.*)

B: Right then. Here goes. I hope . . . (*Closing his eyes, he throws his films into the air with great effort. He opens his eyes, sees they've disappeared and is visibly relieved.*) Oh . . . great! (*Turns to* SR, *smiling.*) Right . . . (*Walks slowly to* SR, *stops, turns, casts a sympathetic but helpless glance at* A, *then walks back towards* SR *and freezes about to ascend, smiling.*)

BAD NOOSE, GOOD NOOSE

With the right treatment this knockabout sketch can be surprisingly moving and poignant. Although it is written as a light-hearted take-off of every Wild West film you've ever seen; the audience should be able to see beyond the horseplay to the real feelings which BAD BARNEY experiences, albeit apparently superficial at first. It is vital that you have a very competent BAD BARNEY who is able to convey those feelings within the context of the play but without appearing 'slushy' or sentimental. It is also vital that you have a very good singer to maintain the background 'blues' theme throughout. A good resonant voice that carries well is a must. Avoid amplification for this at all costs – but if you must, it is essential that the balance is correct so the actors are not drowned out. The hanging scene at the end requires frequent, accurate and precise rehearsal. During the first half, until BAD BARNEY is put into jail, the pace should proceed at almost a gallop. But by the time we get to the end we have come down through a trot to a thoughtful, slow walk. So, saddle up and off you go . . .

The sketch has a wide age appeal (from 10 years to adults) and is useful for almost any situation – but not street theatre.

CHARACTERS: SHERIFF DUCK – Bungling, apparently incompetent, lazy and a coward deep down. (He has elements of 'Boss Hog' from the 'Dukes of Hazzard' – but much more likeable and friendly.) Able suddenly to exert effective cunning and skill – but only once a day . . .

SHIRLEY-MAY – Wide-eyed, prissy but has a sharp edge. Impatient with SHERIFF DUCK.

BAD BARNEY – Mean. Proud. The ultimate 'bad guy'. Enjoys scaring people. But inside he's got true feelings, folks . . .

STRANGER – Male. Preferably with mime skills.

SINGER – Need not necessarily be an actress. Never appears on stage unless you decide that she can also be the:

EXTRA – An important role. Must be costumed for her/his brief appearance. Provides all offstage effects – drumbeats, gunshots, 'spittoon' noises.

All characters wear jeans and checked shirts or T-shirts, donning hats, neckerchiefs and guns as appropriate. SHERIFF DUCK wears a sheriff's badge.

We hear a haunting blues theme OS. SHERIFF DUCK *is seated* SR *rocking on an ordinary chair and snoring with his hat over his eyes. There is another chair* MSL.

SHIRLEY: (*off*) Sheriff! (*He snores. She appears* SL. *Her shouts get louder.*) Sheriff! (*He snores again.*) Sheriff! (*On this she kicks his chair so he lands forward with a thump!*)

SHERIFF: (*startled, jumping up with gun drawn*) Huh? Okay, don't you move you cattle rustlers, I've got you covered. Huh? (*Looks around bemused.*) Oh. Howdy, Shirley-May. Fancy sneaking up on me like that.

SHIRLEY: (*in a turmoil*) Bad Barney's in town!

SHERIFF: (*sitting*) Oh good, Bad Barney huh?
(*Suddenly jumps up again.*) Bad
Barney!

SHIRLEY: (*to audience*) The meanest, leanest,
gunslinger in the whole Wild West.

SHERIFF: (*panicking*) You just stay there
Shirley-May. (*He begins to exit.*) I'll
go get the Sheriff.

SHIRLEY: Sheriff. (*He carries on.*) Sheriff! (*He
stops and turns.*) You are the Sheriff,
Sheriff!

SHERIFF: I am? Oh. So I am. (*Points to the
badge. To audience, raising his hat.*)
Allow me to introduce myself:
Sheriff James Duck.

SHIRLEY: (*noticing something off, shouts*)
Sheriff Duck!

SHERIFF: (*ducking quickly, frightened*) What
for Shirley-May?

SHIRLEY: (*fed up with his antics*) Oh no, not
that. Come over here.
(*They move* SR) He's just gone past
the window.

SHERIFF: (*looking off*) Well, I don't see
nothing.

SHIRLEY: (*to audience*) The mean viper!

SHERIFF: (*to audience*) The sly sidewinder!
When Bad Barney's in town you can
hear him yellin' 'You've had your
beans, mister!' – it sure puts the wind
up them.

BAD BARNEY: (*off, shouts loudly*) You've had
your beans, mister! (*We hear two
'gun' shots, a starting pistol will
suffice. There is a scream, a loud
shout and* BAD BARNEY *enters* SL.)

Well howdy there, Sheriff. (*He
audibly gathers saliva then mimes
spitting* SL *over his shoulder. There is
the 'ping' of a 'spittoon', effects off.*)

SHIRLEY: Well I think it's about time I was
going, Sheriff. (*Exits hastily* SR.)

SHERIFF: Okay, Shirley-May, I'll see yar. (*He
looks round, but she has gone. Terror
grips him, he tries a smile.*) Howdy,
Bad Barney. Nice of you to drop by.
(BARNEY *spits again. 'Spittoon' effect.
Trying to make polite conversation.*)
Wh . . . wh . . . what you been doing
with yourself? B . . . B . . . B . . .
Barney? Heh heh!

BARNEY: (*abruptly*) Funny you should ask me
that, Sheriff. (SHERIFF's *smile
disappears instantly.*) I held up a
stagecoach, shot your deputy, burnt
down thirty-four towns, rustled
myself six thousand head of cattle,
broke out of jail, smashed up the
saloon. And that was before
breakfast. (*Gives an evil smile.*
SHERIFF *gives a nervous
'I'm-trying-hard-to-laugh' laugh.*)
And right now Sheriff I want you to
open up your safe and turn over
every last cent you got (*threatening*
SHERIFF) . . . or else. (*He turns away
smiling.*)

SHERIFF: (*gulping loudly, setting his badge, he
thus summons up mock bravery*) I
ain't goin' to do that Barney.

BARNEY: (*shouts*) What! (SHERIFF *squeals.*)
You cotton-pickin', sidewinding,
buck-bellied, two-toed, son of a
weasel's mother's uncle. I'll tell you

what you can't do. (*During this he has drawn out a large knife. He makes a thrust for* SHERIFF DUCK'*s chest.* SHERIFF DUCK *has long since closed his eyes, fearing the worst.* SHIRLEY-MAY *appears* SR *just in time.*)

SHIRLEY: Sheriff Duck! (*He does so. The knife goes harmlessly over his head.* SHERIFF *immediately springs back up, knocking the knife out of* BAD BARNEY'*s hand.* BAD BARNEY *looks at his hand puzzled.* SHERIFF *nips under* BARNEY'*s legs causing him to look under, then turn round. As he does so* SHERIFF *delivers a powerful uppercut.* BARNEY *provides the 'slap' effect and rocks on his heels – giving a simpering, cross-eyed smile and wave to the audience. He falls backwards slowly, stiff as a board.*)

SHERIFF: Okay, over to you, Shirley-May. (*She catches him under the arms.*) Okay, I've got you now. (*He takes* BARNEY'*s gun away then grabs his feet. They pick him up and move* SL *to the chair.*) Over here. (BARNEY *struggles and shouts. They plonk him down.*) We're going to have a hanging in this town, Barney, and you are going to be at the end of that rope. (*Laughs with relish. During this* SHIRLEY-MAY *has retrieved the knife.*)

BARNEY: (*rising suddenly*) But haven't you forgotten just one little thing Mr Lawman?

SHERIFF: (*terrified again; remembers, almost too late, to point the gun at* BARNEY) Er . . . what's that Barney?

BARNEY: Don't a man get a fair trial around these parts?

SHERIFF: Dagnabit! (*to audience*) I knew I was forgetting something. Okay. Well, you can have a fair trial I guess. Well now, er . . . let me see. Shirley-May, I want you to be the jury (*he points at her with the gun*), and I'll be the judge.
(*Realises he is pointing at himself with the gun.*) Oops! Heh, heh, heh.
(*They form a quick line DS of chairs, facing audience, BARNEY in middle. During the following their heads turn rapidly from audience to each other and back, providing a visual rhythm to go with the words. Work out your own timing for this.*) Okay. Court is in session. Hear ye, hear ye. Jury, how do you find him?

SHIRLEY: Guilty!

SHERIFF: Guilty! How do you plead?

BARNEY: Not guilty!

SHERIFF: Not what? (*Putting his hand to his ear as if not hearing.*)

BARNEY: Guilty.

SHERIFF: Guilty! Yeeeeeeeeeee ha! (SHERIFF and SHIRLEY-MAY *slap knees.*) We're going to have a hanging in this town! A one, a two, a one, two, three, four . . . (*They sing the following to the tune 'De Camptown Races' and perform a hornpipe, side-stepping dance, incorporating some quick turns and jumping kicks. The overall effect should leave the audience and BARNEY surprised. It starts and ends abruptly, returning to the 'natural'*

SHERIFF: (*script.*) Skip to my loo and slap my knee.

ALL: Do da, do da.

SHERIFF: Gonna hang Bad Barney from the highest tree!

ALL: Do da, do da day.
Gonna dance all night, gonna sing all day.

BARNEY: It'll be the death of me.

SHERIFF: You've had your beans.

SHERIFF & S-M: Hooray!

SHERIFF: (*draws gun on* BARNEY) Okay, Barney, into the jail-house with you. (BARNEY *walks towards 'jail'* DSR *at gunpoint. He stops.*)

BARNEY: You better know what you're doing. (*Spits towards* SL. *There is no noise.*) Just ain't my lucky day. (*They continue walking. Spittoon 'pings'. All three do a double-take towards* SL BARNEY *shrugs it off, he goes in jail.* SHERIFF *mimes sliding a jail door closed, locks it and puts the 'key' in his pocket.*)

SHERIFF: (*gleeful chuckle*) You stay put Barney . . . better get yourself plenty of sleep. (*To audience.*) It'll be the last he has. (*He laughs then 'rocks' on chair asleep as before, hat over eyes. The music begins and continues throughout* BARNEY'S *speech. He is still for a while before speaking. He becomes more earnest as speech goes on.*)

BARNEY: Almost sunrise. Oh well, Barney Boy, looks like it's the end of the road for you . . . soon be shooting buffalo in that big prairie up there in

the sky. Only trouble is partners . . .
I don't know if I'm ready to meet my
Maker. I guess, for the first time in
my whole life . . . I guess . . . I'm
scared. (*Music finishes.* SHERIFF
snores.)

SHIRLEY: (*enters* SR) Yaahoooo! (*She hits him
with a black hood.*) Mornin', Sheriff.

SHERIFF: What you doin' here so early,
Shirley-May!

SHIRLEY: We got a hanging this morning,
Sheriff. (*Passes him hood.*)

SHERIFF: Oh sure. We got ourselves Bad
Barney.

SHIRLEY: That's right.

SHERIFF: Here, Shirley-May, you keep him
covered, okay? (*Gives her gun.*) And
I'll fetch him out of the jail-house.
(*Mimes unlocking and opening
door.*) Okay then, Barney, I want
you to come outa there. None of
your tricks now . . . (*Pause.* BARNEY
has not moved.) Well come on now,
Barney. What's the matter with you,
boy? (*Laughs.*) You scared or
something?

BARNEY: (*defensive*) I ain't scared of nothing,
Sheriff. (*He moves out of jail to*
SHERIFF.)

SHERIFF: Ah ha! That sounds more like it,
Barney! Okay, Shirley-May, you
know what to do now. (SHIRLEY-MAY
moves SR *to 'cover'* BARNEY *and takes
his hat off.*) You'd better take a last
look at this world . . . boy. (*He puts
the hood over* BARNEY'S *head. A drum
beat is heard from off at slow, regular
intervals.* SHERIFF *'ties'* BARNEY'S

hands behind his back. BARNEY *is led to chair* SL. BARNEY *steps up on to chair.* SHERIFF *mimes putting a noose round* BARNEY's *head and draws it tight.* SHERIFF *takes off his hat. The drum beat stops with reverence.*) And may God have mercy on your soul.

EXTRA: (*rushing on* SL *in a great panic*) Stop the hanging! Stop the hanging!

SHERIFF: (*angry*) What in tarnation is going on now!

EXTRA: I'm not too late am I, Sheriff?

SHERIFF: Can't you see we've got a hanging here?

EXTRA: But I gotta urgent message for you.

SHERIFF: Urgent huh? . . . (*resigned*) Okay . . . okay . . . (*goes over to* BARNEY.) Just hang on there, Barney. (*Goes back to messenger.*) What is it? (*Message is whispered in* SHERIFF's *ear.*) But why? (*More whispering.*) Are you sure?

EXTRA: Yup.

SHERIFF: (*gives a 'well-if-you-say-so' look*) Okay. I'll be right with you. (EXTRA *exits* SL. SHERIFF *returns to* BARNEY *and begins removing the noose.*) Okay, Barney, I want you to step down from there. There's been a slight change of plan, d'yer hear me? I want you to stand over here out of harm's way, and stay put d'yer hear? (*He moves* BARNEY DSR. SHIRLEY-MAY *follows.*) Shirley-May, I want you to keep him covered. (*Gives* SHIRLEY-MAY *his gun.*) I'll be right back. (*Exits* SL.)

BARNEY: Doggone it! . . . What's goin' on

around here?

SHIRLEY: I dunno, Bad Barney.

BARNEY: Hey, take this thing off my head will
ya?

SHIRLEY: Well . . . I don't see how it'll do any
harm.
(*Enter* SHERIFF *and* STRANGER,
wearing identical black hood.)

SHERIFF: Okay then, mister. Come on this
way. Are you sure you wanna go
through with this? (STRANGER *nods.*)
Okay. (*Drum beat resumes. Repeat
ritual exactly as before, except this
time hands are left loose.* BARNEY *and*
SHIRLEY-MAY *look on from* DSR.
SHERIFF *removes his hat again.*) And
may God have mercy on your soul.
(SHERIFF *draws chair away as drum
sounds a rapid, loud burst of beats.*
STRANGER *jumps off chair and lands
on floor. His body jolts back upward
signifying the rope tightening. Then
he swings, gently sways with his head
at an angle, feet slightly apart – He
could try putting all his weight on one
leg, the same side his head is angled
towards, and swinging the opposite
foot and arm as though limp; this
requires skill and practice – there is a
long pause as we see* SHERIFF *slowly
regaining his composure. All three
characters must appear genuinely
moved.* SHERIFF *crosses to* BAD
BARNEY, *finding it hard to take his
eyes off the* STRANGER.) Okay, Barney.
Shirley-May . . . (*He takes* BARNEY's
*hood from her, folds it up and puts
it in his pocket.*) You're free to go.

BARNEY: (*genuinely amazed*) What? . . . What did you say?

SHERIFF: You heard me, boy. You're free to go. (SHERIFF *'unties'* BARNEY *and hands him his gun.*) Now come on, here's your gun. Shirley-May. (*He takes his gun off her and stows it in his holster or belt.*)

BARNEY: Now wait a minute. What's going on? One minute you're going to hang me, the next minute you turn me loose. I don't understand.

SHERIFF: Well, it's like this, Barney. (*He takes his hat off as if in memory. He appears affected by what has happened but must not 'send it up'.*) You see, a stranger rode into town today and he's been hung instead.

BARNEY: Instead of what?

SHERIFF: Instead of you.

BARNEY: Why, what did he do?

SHERIFF: Well, nothing. Innocent as far as I could tell.

BARNEY: Well, if he was innocent, then . . . why did you go and hang him?

SHERIFF: (*some slight fear of Barney returning*) That's the darndest thing about it. He said something about a new law. He said *he* had to die in your place. (*Taps* BARNEY *on the chest.*) I never heard of it. But I *knew* he was right. (*Looks to audience.*) And he said, 'That's the way it *had* to be'. (*All turn to look at* STRANGER. *Pause.*) Darndest thing I've ever seen . . . well, ha, ha, ha, ha. (*Chuckles.*) Come on, Shirley-May, you live and you learn don't ya? (*Starts to exit.*)

Should've been you hanging up
there, Barney.
(*Exeunt.* BARNEY *looks at the body of
the* STRANGER. *Blues theme from off.
Pause.* SHERIFF *re-enters and mimes
undoing noose.* STRANGER *slumps
down over* SHERIFF's *shoulder and is
carried off.* SHERIFF *pauses to look at*
BARNEY *then exits* SL. BARNEY *reflects,
tries to snap himself out of it as he
puts his hat back on, pauses again
then exits* SR *as the music ends.*)

MY WAY

Whether or not you enjoy Frank Sinatra, or anyone else for that matter, singing the vastly oversung 'My Way', a Christian must admit that the sentiments are certainly suspect. With this in mind the question is posed 'Is there such a thing as living life my way?' A quick look at Matthew 6:24 gives Jesus's view on the matter. This sketch attempts to show such conflict in everyday terms. It has proved useful in church services, school assemblies and youth clubs although it can leave a rather negative feel which needs the positive balance of, perhaps, 'Bad Noose, Good Noose' (page 178) to follow.

CHARACTERS: GOOD – Lively and enthusiastic, finds EVIL constantly irksome but is friendly towards MAN and the audience. Wears gold or silver cloak – not too ostentatious.

EVIL – Sly and calculating. Only sparkles when tempting MAN. Cannot tolerate GOOD's presence. Wears black or dark brown cloak.

MAN – Slightly innocent and unsuspecting but soon becomes selfish. Modern casual dress.

Two chairs are placed DSR *and* DSL. MAN *lying on floor* CS *having been carefully covered with a large black cloth either by* GOOD *and* EVIL *or by two other stage hands. This should be accomplished, hopefully, without the audience's seeing.* MAN *takes his place. (The cloth may be held vertically to obscure his entrance).* GOOD *stands* USL *with back towards the audience.* EVIL *in similar manner* USR *until his first cue.*

> (GOOD *leaps on to chair.*)
>
> GOOD: I'm the servant of good. Good is God, and I'm here for good . . . if you see what I mean.
> (EVIL *leaps on to his chair.*)
>
> EVIL: And I'm the servant of evil, here simply to prove that evil is good!
>
> GOOD: (*indignant*) Good is good!
>
> EVIL: Bad is good!
>
> GOOD: Good is good!
>
> BOTH: Good!
>
> GOOD: My boss made the whole wide world.
>
> EVIL: My boss rules the whole wide world.
>
> GOOD: My boss made both day and night.
>
> EVIL: My boss is a frightful sight.
>
> GOOD: My boss can do all things well.
>
> EVIL: My boss is the King of Hell!
>
> GOOD: (*proudly*) My boss has created man.
>
> EVIL: My boss has . . . er . . . (*defeated*) er, hasn't quite done that yet. But give me a man and we'll see whose boss is boss!
>
> GOOD: Right! So the servant of good springs into action . . . BOINK!
> (*Jumps down from chair and runs behind* MAN *under cloth.*)
> . . . and unveils his boss's greatest creation . . . ladies and gentlemen!
> (*Takes hold of corner of cloth and pulls it away sharply.*)
> Man!
> (*He discards cloth.* MAN *immediately turns to sit facing audience, acting as a baby with ear-piercing screams.*

*Looks at thumb and sticks it in his
mouth. He is silent.* GOOD *and* EVIL
stand on chairs again.)

EVIL: (*sarcastically*) Man?

GOOD: Well, apparently they all start life
like this.
(*To* MAN.) Coochie coochie coo.
Right . . .

BOTH: (*announcing*) Off to school!
(GOOD *claps.* MAN *immediately gets
up, he becomes a young schoolboy
brandishing a catapult.* GOOD *and* EVIL
*get down from chairs and come to
stand either side of* MAN. *They have
also become schoolboys.*)

MAN: 'Ere look! I'm gonna get teacher with
my catapult!

GOOD: Hang on . . . my dad says you've got
to respect your elders . . .

MAN: (*pushing him away*) Oh shut up!

EVIL: Get her right on the bum!

MAN: No! Shut up both of you! I'm gonna
do it my way . . . right on her bum!
(*He mimes firing catapult.*)
Yeah! I got her! I got her!
(GOOD *claps.* MAN *freezes.* GOOD *and*
EVIL *stand on chairs.*)

EVIL: (*scornfully*) That wasn't a very good
start!

GOOD: Well he's young . . . hasn't
developed a conscience yet. Give
him time . . .

BOTH: We'll see.

GOOD: Right . . .

BOTH: (*announcing*) Adolescence!
(GOOD *claps.* MAN *turns and looks at
imaginary motorbike positioned
between chairs.*)

MAN: Wow! What a bike!
(*The following dialogue is in the style of a salesman's patter.*)

BOTH: Welcome to Sid Sprockett's motorbikes!

GOOD: The best bikes.

EVIL: For the best people.

GOOD: Good morning, sir!

EVIL: Good morning, sir!
(MAN *acknowledges, then mimes sitting on bike, etc.*)

GOOD: Why not sit on it?

EVIL: Try it for size.

GOOD: Seven-fifty c.c. engine.

EVIL: A hundred and forty miles an hour.

GOOD: Full chrome exterior.

EVIL: Shaft drive.

GOOD: Four cylinders.

EVIL: Four carburettors.

GOOD: Two thousand . . .

EVIL: Three hundred . . .

GOOD: And twenty . . .

EVIL: Three . . .

GOOD: Pounds.

BOTH: What a bargain!

MAN: Wow! What a bike!
(EVIL *jumps off chair to land on bike behind* MAN.)

EVIL: Two thousand, three hundred and twenty-three pounds? It could be yours for nothing! Look! The keys are in it; you could just drive it out of the shop. It's yours!

GOOD: (*jumping down*)
You'd never get away with it! Okay, two thousand, three hundred and twenty-three may be a lot of money . . . but a few extra hours' overtime,

a few extra days' work . . . it could
be yours. You could save up for it.

EVIL: Nick it!
(MAN *weighs up what they've said,
then climbs off bike.*)

MAN: No! Shut up! Both of you. I'm going
to do it my way . . . I'll save up for it.
(MAN *walks towards back of stage.*
GOOD *claps.* MAN *freezes.* GOOD *and*
EVIL *stand on chairs again.*)

GOOD: (*scornfully*) Who'd steal a bike in
broad daylight?

EVIL: I would.

GOOD: Yes, I know *you* would. (*Sighs.*)
Right!

BOTH: (*announcing*) Manhood!
(GOOD *claps.* MAN *picks up chair from
back of stage and brings it to midway
between* GOOD *and* EVIL. *He sits and
mimes working at office desk.*)

GOOD: Twenty-three years old.

EVIL: Six foot one.

GOOD: Working in an office.

EVIL: Married

GOOD: Two children.

EVIL: Three cats.

GOOD: Lots of responsibilities.

EVIL: And lots of problems.

BOTH: Time to talk.

GOOD: It's time he knew who we are.

EVIL: Good idea.
(*They both sit on backs of chairs.*
GOOD *and* EVIL *both lean forward and
wave, trying to catch* MAN's *attention.*
EVIL *coughs.* GOOD *coughs.* MAN
coughs. GOOD *and* EVIL *whistle or* 'Oi'
loudly.)

MAN: (*jumps, noticing* GOOD *and* EVIL *for*

the first time)

Blimey! What's going on . . .

GOOD: It's all right . . . don't worry . . . you see – I'm the servant of good.

EVIL: And I'm the servant of evil.

BOTH: You're in the story . . .

EVIL: (*pointing to* GOOD)
Of good

GOOD: (*pointing to* EVIL)
And of evil.
(*Pause.*)

MAN: Huh . . . (*Tries to laugh it off.*) what a load of rubbish!
(*Pause, then realising*) . . . Oh! Are you collecting for charity?
(*Feels in pockets.* GOOD *and* EVIL *despair.*)

GOOD: No, look let me explain. I've been sent from on high.

EVIL: And I've been sent from below.

MAN: Eh?
(*During the following,* EVIL *comes down from the chair, unnoticed, to stand behind the* MAN. GOOD *approaches* MAN.)

GOOD: You see . . . my boss would love to help. Help you with your problems.

MAN: Problems? What problems?

GOOD: Your fears, for example. You're frightened of the dark . . . you're frightened of dying . . .
(MAN, *indignant, tries to interrupt.*)
. . . most people are, don't deny it. You see, the fact of the matter is, my boss would love to help you.
(*Pause.*)

MAN: No. No, I'm sorry. I'm not interested.

(MAN *tries to carry on with his work.*)

GOOD: (*whispering in his ear*) He sometimes gives more than one chance.

MAN: Look, I *said* I wasn't interested . . . would you mind leaving me alone!

GOOD: All right, have it your own way.
(*He walks* USC *and stands with back to audience.*)

MAN: Both of you . . .
(*Turns to* EVIL's *chair and stops because* EVIL *is no longer there. Turns back to* GOOD's – *he also has disappeared.*)
Huh!
(*Carries on with work – but then throws down pen despondently.*)

EVIL: (*standing behind* MAN)
You're fed up with your job.

MAN: I'm fed up with my job.

EVIL: You could be a success.

MAN: I *could* be a success.

EVIL: You could be rich.

MAN: (*standing, caught up in dream*)
I could be rich.

EVIL: You *could* be famous.

MAN: (*jumps on to chair*)
I could be famous.

EVIL: You *are* famous.

MAN: I *am* famous.
(*The dream is becoming a reality.*)

EVIL: Look at the people.
(*Indicating audience.*)
They love you.

MAN: (*looking at them*)
They *love* me!

EVIL: They adore you.

MAN: They *adore* me.

EVIL: They worship you.

MAN: (*completely self-indulgent*) They *worship* me!

EVIL: I did it my way.

MAN: (*climax – a shout with hands outstretched*) I did it my way!
(EVIL *pushes* MAN *on to floor viciously and pulls chair away.* MAN *freezes, sprawled face down on floor.* EVIL *carries chair to back of stage, laughing savagely. The laugh is cut off as* EVIL *slams the chair down.* EVIL *next to* GOOD *also with back to the audience. Brief freeze –* GOOD *and* EVIL *turn together and pick up discarded cloth. They unfold it and slowly lower it over* MAN.)

GOOD: (*sighing*) Ashes to ashes.

EVIL: Dust to dust.

GOOD: If God won't have you . . .

EVIL: . . . the devil must.

GOOD: I tried to show him the truth, but he would insist on doing it his way.

EVIL: No! He did it my way.
(*Both freeze.*)

DIRTY RAG

In order to get into the mood of this it is necessary to recall, or better still to watch, some of those delightfully innocent 1940s films in which all the actors talk terribly well, terribly sincerely and terribly fast:

'Will you marry meh Pem?'

'Of course I will Friddie!'

Then the music swells dramatically, a newspaper re-volves on the screen at top speed suddenly stopping to reveal its headline as the music builds to a crescendo.

'Dirty Rag' must be imagined in this genre, the NARRATOR providing all incidental 'music'. He is the one who holds the whole piece together and to a large extent determines its pace. (He is also akin to the token American in the film to assure its sales across the water!) He must work hard at impersonating the sounds of various musical instruments and moods; there is a lot of scope here for inventiveness. Close attention needs to be given to the rhythm through-out. It should be brisk but not breakneck. Movements are stylised and very precisely staged, especially where they fit with the rhythm.

It is not accidental that this piece bears some re-semblance to Matthew 18: 23–35.

CHARACTERS: NEWS VENDOR – An apparent idiot. Relishes his street cry. Wears scruffy clothes and hat. Carries a bundle of papers.

NARRATOR – A very sincere, deter-mined American reporter. Wears private investigator-type mac with large, up-turned collar.

GINNY SCOOP – Immensely sincere, well-spoken, bespectacled young woman. Well dressed. Feels things 'ferreh deepleh'.

JOE MUNGER – A shambling, scruffy, conniving editor-cum-criminal, complete with eyeshade and sleeve suspenders. A chainsmoker (a mock cigarette will suffice).

CHIEF – A no-messing, straight-down-the-line, Scots editor. Tough but not unfeeling.

A table is set at an angle USR *with one chair behind it and another beside it* CS. *Enter* NEWS VENDOR DSL. *He limps and shouts unintelligibly with a raucous wail.*

VENDOR: Reeeeaw wow! Reeeeaw wow! (*Enter* NARRATOR *to* DSC. *He tries to speak to audience.*) Reeeeaw wow! (NEWS VENDOR *continues his slow, purposeful approach to* CS. NARRATOR *glances at him, slightly annoyed, attempts to speak again.*) Reeeeaw wow!

NARRATOR: I beg your pardon?

VENDOR: (*looking at him as if he is a fool*) Reeeeeeeeeeaw . . . wow!

NARRATOR: What did you say?

VENDOR: (*he leans right over to* NARRATOR's *face. Offended*) Read! All! About! It! (*Both look at audience with respective reactions.*) Reeeaw wow! (*He continues his progress* SR *fading volume as he exits.*) Reeeeaw wow! Reeeeeeeaw wow!

NARRATOR: Read all about it! Read all about it! My name is Grubb. Larry Grubb.

I'm a reporter with the *Dirty Rag*,
circulation seven hundred and going
down. I'm standing outside the
offices of the *Dirty Rag*. On the face
of it they look like any other ordinary
dirty office block . . . only dirtier.
(*As he moves* DSL SCOOP *and* MUNGER
*enter very briskly. They sit in their
respective chairs at exactly the same
time.*) Inside behind those warmly lit
curtains sits Joe Munger, the editor,
cooking up some scandal . . . (*He
looks abruptly across at them.*)

SCOOP: I still don't know why you wanted to
see me, Joe . . .

MUNGER: Listen, Ginny Scoop . . .

SCOOP: (*looks quickly to audience, aside*)
Otherwise known as Auntie Bron,
famous problem page writer. (*Looks
quickly back at* MUNGER.)

MUNGER: It's about our newspaper.

SCOOP: (*jumping up*) If you think I'm ever
going to write for your newspaper,
you are very much mistaken. It's
nothing but a dirty rag full of filthy,
pornographic rubbish! (*She sits as if
stressing the point. At the same
moment* MUNGER *is on his feet.*)

MUNGER: (*walks out from behind his desk*)
There's nothing wrong with my
newspaper.

SCOOP: Then why is your circulation so bad?

MUNGER: (*looks at his legs*) That's just the
way I walk. Listen, Ginny, I want to
talk to you about . . . some scandal.

SCOOP: I'm sorry, Joe, but you know I never
divulge any of my client's secrets.

MUNGER: Ah, but what if I was to tell you that

this scandal involved a problem-page
writer?

NARRATOR: (*to audience; a suitable snippet of
tense film music*) Daa-da! (*Looks
back to action.*)

MUNGER: Who goes to Brighton every
weekend . . .

NARRATOR: (*to audience; up in pitch*) Daa-da!
(*Looks back.*)

MUNGER: Telling her husband she's working on
a story . . .

NARRATOR: (*to audience; higher still*) Daa-da!
(*Looks back.*)

MUNGER: When all the time she's having an
affair with another man!

NARRATOR: (*to audience; resolves with emphasis*)
Dan-da-da-da da-da-da-da . . .
da-dum! (*Looks back to action.*)

SCOOP: (*jumps up*) You can never prove
this Joe!

MUNGER: Oh, I have some jolly nice
photographs which just might . . .
Ginny. (*Relishing her obvious agony.*)

SCOOP: What do you want from me?

MUNGER: Listen, Ginny, I want two thousand
pounds from you. And I want it by
tonight. And if I don't get it . . .
you're going to see your face on
tomorrow's front page. (*She is
horrified.*) The rest of you will appear
on page three. (*She looks aghast at
audience. They freeze momentarily.*)

NARRATOR: (*to audience. Excitement-is-
mounting-music.* SCOOP *exits as he
sings,* MUNGER *moves to his desk.*)
Dan da-da-daa! Dan-da-da-
daa! Da dum! (*Mimes a telephone,
looks at* MUNGER.) Brringg brringg!

Brringg bringg! Brin . . . (MUNGER
picks up a 'telephone'.) Five minutes
later Joe Munger receives a
telephone call from . . . the Chief.
The Chief is the boss of Good News
Press, owners of five leading
newspapers . . . and the *Dirty Rag*.
He wants to talk with Munger, and
talk with him fast! (*Exciting
what's-going-to-happen-next?-Type
music*) Diddle iddle da dum. Diddle
iddle da dum, etc. (*During this*
MUNGER *rises and moves* USC. CHIEF
*enters with newspaper and sits behind
desk. The movement is quick and
precise, starting and finishing in time
with the music.*) Da dum! Ten
minutes later Joe Munger is knocking
on the Chief's office door. (*Looks
back to action.*)

MUNGER: (*'knocking'*) Knock, knock, knock.
CHIEF: Come in!
MUNGER: (*entering 'door'*) You wanted to
speak to me, Chief?
CHIEF: Ah, Munger. I won't mince my
words. It's about your newspaper.
(*Fingering it as though infested.*)
MUNGER: Ah . . . yes. Perhaps we could
discuss this over a cup of tea . . .
(*makes as if to escape.*)
CHIEF: Sit down, Munger! (*As he does so*
CHIEF *rises.*) Never in all my
twenty-five years of working with the
Good News Press have I seen a more
despicable, filthy, low-down piece of
rubbish! (*Slams the paper down.*) I
wouldn't even wrap my haggis in it!
MUNGER: Aah . . . we've been going through

something of a bad patch recently
. . . um . . .

CHIEF: Bad patch?! I don't call seven years a
bad patch! Just look at today's
offering. (*He flicks through it.*) Front
page: 'M.P. drops his trousers'. Page
two: 'Minister drops his trousers'.
Page three: (*eyes almost pop*) Ugh!
Page four: (*incredulous*) 'Naked mud
wrestling at the Derby and Joan
club'? Back page sport: 'Referee
drops his shorts'!

MUNGER: But there were some very good
photographs . . .

CHIEF: I'm not interested in your excuses,
Munger! Either I wrap up your
newspaper or I wrap you up!

MUNGER: Is that your final word on the matter?

CHIEF: It is!

MUNGER: Very well. (*Jumps up.*) You leave me
with only one alternative! (*Pause. We
get the impression he is scheming
something else.*) To beg for mercy
. . . (*He grovels convincingly as*
NARRATOR *provides a mimed violin
playing* 'Hearts and flowers' *full of
pathos.*) Please I beg you,
reconsider! I'll clean up the
newspaper! I'll even clean myself up!
Oh, please . . . etc.

CHIEF: (*convinced by all the trouser-leg
tugging*) All right, Munger . . . (*he
realises the 'violin' is still playing. He
makes a 'cut' sign to* NARRATOR, *who
stops, smiles apologetically, then
adopts his serious narrator attitude
again.*) I've had time to reconsider.
There's a motto in this company

which says: 'If anyone is willing to change their ways, then we are willing to forgive and forget.' So if you clean up your newspaper, get rid of all the smut, all the rubbish, all the blackmail . . . we'll let you stay on and start again. (MUNGER, *delighted, makes as if to hug him.*) But remember! This is your last chance! Don't mess it up!

MUNGER: (*hugging him, much to* CHIEF's *repugnance*) Oh thank you! Thank you! You won't regret this, Chief, I promise you! This is a new lease of life! (*They both freeze momentarily.*)

NARRATOR: (*to audience*) Read all about it! Editor receives new lease of life! (*He provides more exciting music, during which* MUNGER *and* CHIEF *exeunt and* SCOOP *enters and sits* USR, *pen in hand and her glasses on the desk in front of her. It is all timed to the music.*) Meanwhile, over the other side of town Ginny Scoop, alias Auntie Bron famous problem-page writer, faces a crisis. She can solve other people's problems – but can she solve her own? (*Looks back to action.*)

SCOOP: (*worried and tense, she is writing*) Dear Auntie Bron . . . I have a slight problem. I've been having an affair with another man. It's all over now of course and I'll never see the man again. But someone has found out . . . (*she begins to lose control*) and they're going to tell my husband and everyone else unless I can find two thousand pounds by tonight! What

can I do? I . . . am . . . desperate!
(*Pause. She picks up her glasses and
puts them on. She is confident and
controlled and uses her professional,
understanding voice. She writes
again.*) Dear Desperate. Tell . . .
your . . . husband. (*Whips glasses
off, panic.*) I can't do that, he'd kill
me! (*Puts glasses back on. Controlled
again. Still writing.*) Pay . . . the . . .
money. (*Whips glasses off.*) Where
on earth am I going to get two
thousand pounds? (*She has an idea.
Glasses back on as before.*) If I were
you . . . I would beg for mercy . . .
(*glasses off again*) I could never,
never beg for mercy! (*Freeze.*)

NARRATOR: (*to audience*) Twenty minutes later
she was to beg for mercy! (*He
provides* 'The-Plot-Thickens' *music
as* SCOOP *moves away from the table
and* MUNGER *enters;* SCOOP *is on her
knees.*)

SCOOP: Please, Joe, reconsider!

MUNGER: No chance, Ginny. Oh . . . I can see
the headlines now. (*He moves* DS.)
Personal Problems of a Problem-
page Writer!

NARRATOR: (*to audience*) Read all about it!
Personal Problems of a Problem-
page Writer! (*Looks back to action.*)

SCOOP: (*shuffling on her knees to* MUNGER) I
beg you, Joe, please reconsider.
Think of my husband, my family, my
friends. What will they say? (*She is
weeping.*)

MUNGER: No chance Ginny.

SCOOP: Think of my career. I'll be ruined.

(*She is sobbing and tugging at his trouser leg.*) Please give me a chance to build my life again! (NARRATOR *provides 'violin' and* 'Hearts and flowers' *as before. It is full of emotion.* SCOOP *is sobbing and wailing.*)

MUNGER: (*realising that this has got out of hand, shouts to* NARRATOR *who is now quite carried away*) Shut up! (*Taken by surprise, the* NARRATOR *accidentally screeches and scrapes on the 'violin' with a cacophony of noise. He then resumes his normal serious attitude.* MUNGER *kicks* SCOOP *to the ground.*) Get lost! (*He exits.*)

NARRATOR: (*moves* CS *to* SCOOP.) She was broken-hearted.

SCOOP: (*kneeling up*) I'm broken-hearted.

NARRATOR: She had no one left to turn to.

SCOOP: (*speaking through her tears*) I have no one left to turn to! (*She breaks down and grasps at* NARRATOR's *sleeve, much to his embarrassment. Still sobbing, she 'climbs' up his arm and sobs on his shoulder. He smiles uncertainly. She screams an ear-piercing wail.* NARRATOR *gallantly produces a handkerchief and gives it to her. Through her sobs we almost hear a* 'thank-you'. *She blows her nose loudly.* NARRATOR *jumps.* SCOOP *exits slowly as* NARRATOR *provides a muted-trumpet-type tragic phrase of music.*)

NARRATOR: (*changing the mood suddenly*) Is it curtains for Ginny Scoop? What's in store for Joe Munger? Will the Chief

ever find out? Why do I keep asking
so many questions? Later that day
the Chief receives an anonymous
phone call. Brringg brringg! (CHIEF
enters and picks up the 'telephone'.)
Brringg brri . . . (NARRATOR *provides
an unintelligible falsetto burbling.*)

CHIEF: WHAT?! Send for Joe Munger!
(NARRATOR *provides the-end-is-near
music, ending with two strong beats.
Enter* MUNGER, *in time with the music,
who arrives on the last beat.* CHIEF
stands as he bangs the table.)
Munger! (MUNGER *jumps nervously.*)
I gave you your last chance but you
messed it up! (*Approaching* MUNGER
slowly, driving him SL.) I've heard all
about this scandal, all this blackmail!
You're not fit to work on a
newspaper! You're not fit to be an
editor on the Good News Press!
You're going to be handed over to
the law! (*By now they have reached*
NARRATOR *who grabs* MUNGER *by the
scruff of the neck.*)

NARRATOR: Joe Munger was sentenced to seven
years in prison. (*He takes* MUNGER'*s
eyeshade off him.*) For blackmail.
(*He releases him and* MUNGER'*s head
hangs down.* NARRATOR *moves* SR
putting eyeshade on.) I became editor
of the *Dirty Rag*, only now we call it
. . . (*He half sits on the table.*) . . .
The Sign of the Times. Ginny Scoop?
(*She has entered to* DSC *next to* CHIEF.)
She carried on being a problem page
writer and was the first to advise
women to stick to only one man. The

Chief? (*He has come to life and looks admonishingly at* SCOOP, *who is ashamed*.) Well, he remained a fair man and true to the saying that 'If anyone is willing to change their ways, (SCOOP *shows she is.* CHIEF *smiles benignly*) he is willing to forgive and forget'. (*They all freeze*.)

VENDOR: (*from* OS) Reeeaw wow! (*Enters* SR.) Reeeeaw wow! (*He limps to* MSR.) Reeeaw wow! Actors leave the stage without a punchline! (*Brief pause. Then in a frenzy of activity, not unlike a speeded-up Keystone Kops film, all actors rush off the stage with exaggerated panic, leaving it suddenly empty*.)

THE LOST COIN
(or THERE'S MORE TO THIS THAN
MEETS THE EYE)

This sketch is a con-trick. It can only work effectively if the actors make the audience feel embarrassed that the performance has 'gone wrong' and then later make them suspect that the 'mistakes' were deliberate. This may be achieved by exaggerating the style of acting up to, and following, the contact lens section. It is absolutely essential that the lens sequence is as naturalistic as possible.

CHARACTERS: A&B – The 'we've-seen-them-so-many-times-in-Christian-drama' narrators; they try hard to be witty and skilful, but fail miserably.

LADY – A colourful and enjoyable comedienne who gives her heart and soul to the drama – when it is going well . . .

EXTRA – A walk-on, walk-off, non-speaking part which could be coped with by the world's worst actor, if necessary!

A&B *stand* DSL *and* R *on chairs. The* LADY USC *with back to audience. Table* CS.

A: Jesus told this story.
B: There was once a woman.
   (LADY *moves* DSL. *She smiles*

exaggeratedly to audience.)

A: She had a great, big, fat . . .

B: Leather purse.
   (LADY *produces a 'heavy' bag which she drags to* CS.)

B: And inside it she had . . .

A: Ten silver coins.
   (LADY *looks inside bag, looks up with a big smile.*)

B: Every day she picked up her purse
   . . .
   (LADY *makes a big show of picking up the weight.*)

A: Went to her table . . .
   (LADY *does so and collapses on to it, exhausted.*)

B: Got out the coins . . .

A: And counted them.
   (LADY *produces one silver disc about 30 cm in diameter from the purse and holds it up to the audience.*)

B: One.
   (LADY *slaps the disc down on the table and produces a second from the bag, and so on.*)

A: Two.
   (LADY *as before.*)

B: Three.
   (*The narration gets too fast for the* LADY *to produce the coins in time.* B *develops a twitch in one eye.*)

A: Four.

B: Five.

A: Six.

B: (*beginning to rub his eye and blinking*) Seven.

A: Eight.

B: (*having great difficulty*) Nine.

A: Ten . . .

B: Hang on!

A: Silver . . .

B: Hang on. (A *and* LADY *stop. There is panic in their eyes. During the above the* LADY *has only managed to get out seven silver coins. There is an awkward pause as* B *pokes at his eye.*) I've lost my contact lens.
(*It is at this point that the actors appear to stop acting and break out of the sketch. The audience should begin to feel embarrassed for them.*)

A: (*disbelieving*) Steve? (*or actor's real name*)

LADY: (*very embarrassed*) Steve?

B: I've got to find it. (*Pause.*) I'm sorry. (*He starts examining his clothes carefully then steps down from his chair.*)

LADY: Can't you wait until we get to the end?

A: Yeah, let's just finish the sketch can't we?

B: No I've got to find it. I can't read my script without it.
(*They all give the audience self-conscious apologetic smiles and generally appear uncomfortable as they look on the floor under the furniture and, where possible around the feet of the audience if in close proximity.*)

B: Careful it could be anywhere.

A: Can't you carry on without it?

B: No I need it.

LADY: (*matter of fact*) But it's only a little bit of plastic.

B: But it's worth a lot of money.
(*Resuming the search.*) It's all right!
I've found it! (A *and* LADY *express
relief as* B *mimes picking it up,
sucking it, and putting back into his
eye, which smarts and gives a little
trouble.*)

A: Great!

LADY: (*light-heartedly sarcastic*) Hallelujah!
(*They all return to original positions.*)

B: Right.

LADY: (*checking with them both*) Okay?

B: (*wiping eye*) Yeah.

A: Where were we?
(LADY *counts coins on the table.*)

LADY: . . . five, six, seven . . . the next
one's eight.

A: Right (*to* B) Okay? (B *nods. From this
point the sketch continues as before,
the* LADY *producing coins eight and
nine as they count.*) Eight.

B: Nine.
(LADY *as before*)

A: (*triumphant*) Ten silver coins! (*The*
LADY *is frantically searching her
empty bag, unable to produce the
tenth coin.* A *coughs pointedly.*) Ten
silver coins.

B: Oh dear.

A: She'd lost one.

A&B: Where could it be?
(*The following sequence moves
quickly but only the* LADY *appears to
rush with suitable movements to what
is said.*)

A: She looked high.

B: She looked low.

A: She looked fast.

B: She looked slow.

A: She looked here. (*Points at the floor
in front of his chair.* LADY *rushes to
look.*)

B: She looked there. (*Repeats.*)

A: She looked . . .

A&B: Everywhere. (LADY *shrugs and takes
a deep breath.*)

A: Upstairs . . .

B: And downstairs . . .

A: Around . . .

B: And around . . .

A: Up in the cupboards . . .

B: And down on the ground.

A: She looked . . .

A&B: Everywhere. (LADY *moves* DSC,
shrugs again as if giving up.)

A: (*as if giving big build up*) And then!

B: (*pushes the tenth disc with his foot on
to the floor from his chair where he
has accidentally left it instead of
putting it in the bag, as he presumably
should have done. He is embarrassed
as he tries to cover up this mistake.
With a guilty casualness*) She found
it.

A: (*glaring at* B) She was so pleased.
(LADY, *having picked up the coin,
beams.*)

B: She invited all her friends.
(LADY *beckons imaginary crowd*
US.)

A: And threw a great party.
(LADY *picks up a large (polystyrene)
sign which reads* 'party', *shows it to
the audience and then throws it
offstage with great effort.*)

B: And Jesus said

(LADY *moves* DSC *and hugs the 'lost'
coin.*)

A: In the same way . . .

B: God throws an even bigger party . . .

A: In heaven . . .

B: When one sinner . . .

A: Comes back to him.

(*Brief pause as if the piece has
finished. Then* B *loses his balance
and falls clumsily off his chair.* B
*looks up with a pained expression of
apology.* A *and* LADY *look at* B*, tut
disapprovingly, look at audience and
sigh. A fourth person rushes onstage
and holds up a sign which reads
'applause'. All bow.*)

ii One Act Play

ABOUT FACE

On first reading this play may appear less demanding than it actually is. Much of its success depends upon the atmosphere and mood generated by all three actors and the NARRATOR in particular. MR MAN should have good mime skills and the DUSTMAN a strong stage presence without appearing puppet-like (he has no words). A fairly experienced, or at least enthusiastic, director is essential – as are a striking set of half masks. Suitable music may be used at the beginning and end.

'About Face' is based on the Scripture Union story 'In the Bin' and is used with kind permission and our grateful thanks. We would also like to thank Ronald Mann for his encouragement and advice in developing this piece – any resemblance between him and his namesake in the play is purely coincidental!

> CHARACTERS: MR MAN – Middle-aged, middle-class, office worker.
> NARRATOR – Also dons masks to become WIFE, MISS SPELT, and SCUM.
> DUSTMAN – Earthy but gentle. Strong.

Table, chair and wastebin USL. *Chair* SR. *Chair with newspaper on* DSL. *Briefcase and set of half masks (*MR MAN's*) on floor* CS. NARRATOR *and her masks either* SR *or* SL *just off the main set but visible. Dustbin.*

MR MAN *stands* USC *with back to the audience. Throughout*

the play he mimes actions described by the NARRATOR *who is situated just off set.*

NARRATOR: This is the tale of Mr Man. An ordinary man on an ordinary day. He woke up one morning, stretched and climbed out of bed. He went over to the window to draw back the curtains and find out what kind of day it was.

MR MAN: One, two, three, (*pulls back the curtains.*) Argh! (*looks again.*) It's a miserable day. Miserable.

NARRATOR: Having decided that it was a miserable kind of day he went over to his chest of drawers and pulled open one of the drawers to look at the array of masks lying there.

MR MAN: (*at masks*) Mmmm. Now then, let me see.

NARRATOR: He picked them up one by one. He was trying to decide which would be the right kind of face for a miserable Monday morning.

MR MAN: (*looking at green mask*) Mmm. No, not miserable enough. (*Picks up correct one.*) Yes, this looks like it might do.

NARRATOR: Having chosen one, he put it on and went across to the mirror to make sure that it was in fact miserable enough.

MR MAN: (*miserably*) Good morning. Yes. Yes, that's fine.

NARRATOR: Then he went back to his chest of drawers and, picking out several of the masks, he packed them carefully into his briefcase just in case he might need them during the day. He went out of the bedroom, down the stairs and into the kitchen (DSL) where he sat down at the breakfast table, read his newspaper and ignored his wife. (*Puts on* WIFE *mask. It is worried and slightly haggard.*)

WIFE: 'Morning, dear. Lovely morning.

MR MAN: (*hiding behind paper*) Mmm.

WIFE: Now, one egg or two?

MR MAN: Yes, dear.

WIFE: One egg or two?

MR MAN: (*looks out from paper*) I don't like eggs.

WIFE: Eggs are very good for you. Keep your sunny side up! Now, one egg or two?

MR MAN: Very well, one egg.

WIFE: Two eggs, bacon, sausage, tomato and fried bread. (*She sets 'food' in front of him.*)

MR MAN: Eugh!

WIFE: Now eat it up. It is very good for you.

MR MAN: (*resumes reading*) Yes, dear.

WIFE: (*almost talking to herself*) Oh I do hope it is going to be a nice day. I want to get all of my washing dried.

MR MAN: It is going to rain.

WIFE: Really? Mrs Brown at number sixty-five said it was going to be a lovely day.

MR MAN: (*looking up*) Well, of course, Mrs Brown is the national meteorological office isn't she?

WIFE: No need to be like that. Have you seen the time? Five minutes to your train. You are going to be late.

MR MAN: (*reading*) Yes, dear.

WIFE: You were late yesterday, late the day

before, late the day before that, late
tomorrow, late every day. I don't
know what your boss is going to think
of me. You're going to be late.

MR MAN: (*still reading, yawning*) Yes, dear.

WIFE: You're going to be late.

MR MAN: Oh, my goodness. Look at the time.
Five minutes to my train. I'm going
to be late. I was late yesterday, late
the day before, late the day before
that. What is my boss going to think
of me? Goodbye, dear. (*He folds
the paper up and puts it on the
chair.*)

WIFE: (*she hands him his briefcase*) Have a
good day at the office, dear.

MR MAN: I will. I might. Who knows? Delete
as applicable. (*Brief freeze.*)

NARRATOR: (*takes* WIFE *mask off. Resumes
position*) He went out of the house
and down the street. As he walked
towards the station he saw several of
his friends who were also wearing
their Monday morning faces.

MR MAN: Morning, Matthew. Win at golf on
Saturday? Neither did I. Have a good
weekend? No. Neither did I.
Morning, Roger. Is that the time?
Good heavens!

NARRATOR: He arrived at the station just in time
to catch the train. He climbed on.
There was nowhere to sit. As usual
on a Monday morning he had to
stand. The train set off.

MR MAN: (*jolting forward*) Sorry. (*Looking
round at the 'people'.*) Sorry. Sorry.
(*To himself.*) Dogs shouldn't be
allowed on trains anyway.

(DUSTMAN *enters through audience with dustbin.*)

NARRATOR: He looked around at the faces, the same Monday morning faces that were always there behind their newspapers, and was quite glad when they came to the first station and the train stopped. Further down the carriage someone else climbed on. (DUSTMAN *climbs on. Puts bin down.*) The train set off. (*It jolts.*) Mr Man stared. Everyone stared. It wasn't just that the man was scruffy. It wasn't even that he had a dustbin. He wasn't wearing a mask!

MR MAN: (*spoken as a series of clichés*) Absolutely disgusting. It shouldn't be allowed. What is the world coming to? Tut, tut, tut, tut.

NARRATOR: They were all scandalised and tried to look the other way, at their newspapers or out of the window till the train reached the station and stopped. (*They jolt again.*) Mr Man climbed out, glad to be out of the sight of that awful man. (DUSTMAN *follows* MR MAN *at a distance.*) As he walked down the road towards his office he got that feeling you get when you think that there is someone following you. (*Turns.*) No. No. It must be his imagination. He carried on. But then again, he did think he could hear footsteps. (*Turns.*) No. No. (MR MAN *looks at his watch.*) And he was going to be late. But, yes, there was someone there. Someone following him. It was that man, the

one off the train, the one without the
mask: and he was looking at him.

MR MAN: (*slight panic*) He's following me. I
wonder what he wants? I wonder
what he is after? I know, when I get
to my office, I'll call the police.
(DUSTMAN *sits on the dustbin opposite
to* NARRATOR – *extreme* DSL *or* R.)

NARRATOR: He hurried on to his office, up the
front steps, he pushed the button to
the lift, went in – up to the fifth floor
and out again, along the corridor
and, at last, into the peace and
sanctity of his own little office.

MR MAN: (*sitting*) Ah, the peace and sanctity of
my own little office.

NARRATOR: Where he sat down and, heaving a
sigh of relief, took off his mask. He
picked up his briefcase and carefully
took each mask out, laying it on his
desk, just in case he might need it
during the morning. He was just
about to settle down to some good
hard work . . . (*he nods off*) when
he remembered that he had a new
secretary.

MR MAN: Ah, yes, now I must impress her. Let
me see, which mask shall I wear?
Yes, this looks right. (*Puts on very
happy, enthusiastic mask. His voice
changes accordingly.*) Ha-ha-ha.
'Good morning, my dear.' Yes, I
think that'll do. (*He moves* MSR *where*
NARRATOR *has donned attractive,
young mask and is seated on the chair
miming and making the noises of a
typewriter.*) Hello.

MISS SPELT: Oh!

MR MAN: Hello. I'm your new boss. My name is Mr Man. But you can call me Mr Man. (*They both laugh.*)

MISS SPELT: I'm Miss Spelt (*slightly awkward pause*) Deirdre.

MR MAN: Oh, hello, Deirdre, so pleased to meet you. I hope your stay here is going to be a happy one.

MISS SPELT: Oh, I'm sure it will. I'm going to do everything I can to please you, sir.

MR MAN: (*speculatively*) Everything?

MISS SPELT: Oh, yes, everything.

MR MAN: (*fatherly*) Well, don't work too hard on your first day. (*He makes to go.*)

MISS SPELT: I won't.

MR MAN: (*turning very suddenly*) Ermm . . . how about lunch 12.30?

MISS SPELT: (*mock coyness*) Oh. So soon? Oh well, if you insist . . .

MR MAN: Oh I do, I do. See you then . . . then (*laughs.*) Bye! (*Returns to his office* USL *and takes off his mask.*)

MISS SPELT: Bye! (*Laughs.*)

NARRATOR: (*takes mask off and resumes position*) A few minutes later, someone else arrived at Deirdre's desk. (*Intercom noise.* MR MAN *quickly dons happy mask.*)

MR MAN: Hello, Deirdre, yes?

MISS SPELT: (*without mask, holding nose*) There's someone to see you, sir.

MR MAN: Oh yes. Who is it?

MISS SPELT: She says her name is Scum.

MR MAN: Scum? Ah, yes. Send her in, Deirdre, please.

MISS SPELT: Very well. (NARRATOR *puts on* SCUM *mask with back to audience.*)

MR MAN: (*takes off happy mask*) Now then,

which mask for Scum? Yes, the
miserable one. (*He puts it on and
assumes an 'I'm-the-boss-and-I'm-
waiting' pose.* SCUM *is a downtrodden
underling and obviously nervous.*)

SCUM: Good morning, sir.

MR MAN: What's good about it?

SCUM: (*jumping slightly*) Nothing, sir; it's a
terrible morning.

MR MAN: Now what do you want to see me
about, Scum?

SCUM: It's about the California contract, sir.

MR MAN: Ah, splendid. Good news, I hope?

SCUM: Well actually, no, sir.

MR MAN: What do you mean, 'No, sir'?

SCUM: (*apologetically*) We've lost it, sir.

MR MAN: What do you mean you've lost it?
Can't you even look after a few
sheets of paper?

SCUM: No, sir, not that. We've er . . .
they've er . . . they've cancelled, sir.

MR MAN: Cancelled? What do you mean,
cancelled? After all that hard work *I*
put in?

SCUM: Well, they said, sir, that it was the
weather, sir.

MR MAN: That's not good enough, Scum. I
want to hear every reason. I want a
good explanation and I want it now.
(*He changes the miserable mask for a
red ferocious one.* SCUM *must not see
this.* MR MAN's *physique alters
accordingly.*)

SCUM: (*floundering*) Well, well they said it
was the weather, sir, in California.

MR MAN: (*revelling in his authority*) Get out.
Get out! You're sacked. Fired.
Kaput. Go!

SCUM: But, sir.

MR MAN: Go! (SCUM *exits in tears.* MR MAN *takes off his angry mask and fans himself with it.*)

NARRATOR: Hot from his conquest, he went across to the window to pull up the blind and get a breath of fresh air. He was just about to take a deep breath of carbon monoxide when he noticed (NARRATOR's *voice begins to reflect* MR MAN's *emotional reaction*) there, on the other side of the street, five flights down, that man, the one without the mask, sitting there, looking at him, and now he hadn't got his mask on.

MR MAN: (*hastily putting angry mask back on*) Go away, do you hear me, go away! You've no right sitting there looking into the office windows. Do you hear me, go away before I call the police!

NARRATOR: The man just got up and, shrugging his shoulders, picked up his dustbin and walked sadly away. (DUSTMAN *exits either* SR *or* L.)

MR MAN: (*laughing*) Just shows you what a little bit of authority will do these days. Yes. (*He places mask back on the desk and sits thinking.*)

NARRATOR: A few moments later. (*Makes telephone ringing sound as she puts on* MISS SPELT's *mask.*)

MISS SPELT: Hello? Yes, I'll see if he's free. (*She buzzes him.* MR MAN *snaps into action and quickly puts on the happy mask.*)

MR MAN: Hello, Deirdre.

MISS SPELT: There is someone on the phone for you, sir.

MR MAN: Who is it?

MISS SPELT: I think it is the boss.

MR MAN: Oh yes. Put him on line two. Give me a moment or two. (*He takes off happy mask and puts on self-effacing, grovelling mask.*)

MISS SPELT: Very well, sir. I'm putting you through now, sir. You're through.

MR MAN: (*playing the sycophant for all he is worth*) Hello, sir. (NARRATOR *supplies an unintelligible blabbering by 'blurbing' the lips with fingers.*) Yes, sir? (*Blurbing.*) Couldn't agree more sir. What a lovely morning. (*Blurbing.*) Yes, sir. (*Laughs.*) (*Blurbing.*) Oh, you've made your mind up about the job? Lovely. Yes, sir. (*Blurbing.*) Oh, you've given the job to Johnson? Well, well. (*Disappointed.*) I'm very pleased, sir; yes, sir, very pleased. (*Blurbing.*) Of course I'm not disappointed, sir. We all trust your decisions implicitly. Yes, sir. (*Blurbing.*) Yes, sir, of course. Same time for golf on Saturday, sir? Yes, sir. Yes, sir. Goodbye.
(*Blurbing again but we can almost hear* 'goodbye'. *He puts phone down.*) So. (*He takes off the grovelling mask.*) Johnson got the job did he? It's not fair. (*He puts on the green jealous mask.*) I've been here for twelve years working my fingers to the bone and that baldheaded twit comes from America, been here two years and takes the job that's rightfully mine.

It's not fair. It's just not fair.
(*Suddenly taking his jealous mask off.*)
I know. I'll write him a letter. Yes.
That's what I'll do. (*He swops it for
the happy mask.*) A letter
congratulating him, I think. (*He puts
on the happy mask again and 'buzzes'*
MISS SPELT.)

MISS SPELT: Yes, sir?

MR MAN: Hello, Deirdre.

MISS SPELT: Hello, sir.

MR MAN: Come in and take a letter would you?

MISS SPELT: Right away, sir. (*She puts on her
mask.*)

MR MAN: Very good. (*He smooths his hair,
rubs his shoes on the back of his legs
and poses in an 'I'm-the-affable-
casual-boss' position, half sitting on
his desk.*) Hello, Deirdre.

MISS SPELT: Hello, sir.

MR MAN: To Johnson – eighth floor.
From Man – fifth floor. (*As this letter
progresses it becomes increasingly
sarcastic until it is completely
insincere.*) So pleased to hear of your
recent job promotion. You're
obviously the right man for the job.
Don't work yourself too hard. Can't
have you in the grave after only a few
months, now can we? (*Offhand.*)
Must buy you a drink sometime.
Yours sincerely, Mr Man. That will
be all, Deirdre. (*She starts to leave.
He leers after her.*)

MISS SPELT: Oh, sir. (*She turns, only to catch the
leer momentarily. They exchange
nervous laughs.*) There's someone
else to see you.

MR MAN: Yes, who is it?

MISS SPELT: (*awkward*) Well, he didn't give his name, but he is rather . . . strange . . .

MR MAN: Well, we get all sorts in here you know.

MISS SPELT: (*embarrassed*) He's not . . . well, he hasn't got . . .

MR MAN: (*in an effort to console and relieve*) Well, don't worry, Deirdre. You show him in. I'll deal with him. (*Fatherly again.*) Have you had your coffee break yet?

MISS SPELT: No, sir.

MR MAN: ('*Aren't-I-so-capable-and-in-control*') Well, you go and have your coffee and show this . . . gentleman in.

MISS SPELT: Thank you, sir.

MR MAN: Thank *you*.

MISS SPELT: 'Bye.

MR MAN: Goodbye. (*He goes to desk to swap his mask for the miserable one. He assumes an 'I'm-a-very-busy-boss' pose.* DUSTMAN *has entered* SR *to* MISS SPELT.)

MISS SPELT: This way, he'll see you now. (*She leads* DUSTMAN *into* MR MAN*'s office and sidles out awkwardly.*)

MR MAN: (*looking at 'chart' on the wall*) Come in, come in. I shan't be a moment. I'm a very busy man. Now then, what can I do for . . . (*he turns to discover* DUSTMAN) you! What do you want? What are you doing here? (DUSTMAN *puts bin down between them.*) Take that filthy dustbin out of here this instant! Do you hear me? Go away.

(*It is the* DUSTMAN'S *intention to take* MR MAN'S *masks and put them in the dustbin. Throughout this sequence he confidently, firmly and kindly removes them one by one.*) Go away. What do you want? (DUSTMAN *approaches him.*) No. No. Leave me alone. What do you want? What do you think you're playing at? (DUSTMAN *takes mask off him. Pause.*) Give me that back. (*He realises his face is exposed. He grabs the angry mask.*) Get out of here! What do you think you are doing coming in here, taking things that don't belong to you? You ought to be ashamed of yourself! (DUSTMAN *shakes his head and moves to him slowly.*) Now what do you want? No, you can't have this one! Get out of my way. (*Pushes* DUSTMAN *aside.*) Deirdre, Deirdre, there's a lunatic in my office! Call the police! Quick! (DUSTMAN *takes all the masks left on the desk.* MR MAN *turns.*) Now what do you think you are doing? Put those down. They're mine. (*Pause as they all drop into the bin.*) Give them back to me. (DUSTMAN *comes for angry mask.*) No. No. Please leave me one. (*Pathetically.*) Please leave me with one. (*He is cowering.*) It's all that I've got left. (DUSTMAN *takes angry mask and puts it in the bin. Real anger rises in* MR MAN.) Aren't you satisfied? My God, who do you think you are? Coming in here, taking things that don't belong to

you. (DUSTMAN *heaves the bin up on
to his shoulder*.) That's all my life
you've got in there. What more do
you want? (DUSTMAN *comes towards
him again*.) No. You can't have me.
You can't take me with you! (*He
panics*.) Go away! Go away! Go
away! (*Pushes him violently. He falls
down. Silence. Reflective mood*.) I
remember looking out of the window
and there he was. Five flights down.
Lying on the pavement, not moving.
And there was the dustbin, my masks
and I'd pushed him. It was all my
fault. I felt ill and sick inside . . . that
feeling you get when you know
you've done something completely
irreversible. Something you can't put
right. I'd killed him! (*Pause*.) But my
masks. I had to get my masks back!
(*Turning away*.) I panicked. I turned
and ran for the lift. (*He springs into
action*. DUSTMAN *gets up and exits
leaving only the masks*.) Why doesn't
the lift come when you want it? I'll
have to take the stairs. Five flights of
stairs. No joke when you've got a
stomach ulcer. (*He frantically 'runs'
down the stairs*.) Out of the way!
Stop looking at me. Out of my way!
Excuse me. And then down to
the main entrance. (*Pause. He is
catching his breath, shocked*.) But
when I got there the body was gone
. . . there was nothing left. Just my
masks. My masks! Oh come to daddy
. . . yes, there we are all safe now.
(*Looking up at audience*.) But then

there was a crowd of people all watching me. (*He establishes eye contact.*) All looking at me. (*Puts on ingratiating mask. Laughs.*) It's all right, you can all go home now. Just someone having a practical joke I expect. (*Pause.*) Well didn't you hear me? You can all go. It's all over. Stop looking at me. Leave me alone. (*He retreats into his office, puts the masks on the desk, takes off the one he has on and examines it. Pause.*)

NARRATOR: By now Deirdre had returned from her coffee break and was relieved to find the strange man gone. (*She puts on mask and moves to MR MAN's office.*)

MISS SPELT: I've typed the letter, Mr Man.

MR MAN: What? Oh . . . hello. (*Fumbles for the right mask. He puts the happy mask on but remains flustered.*) Ah . . . ah, hello, Edith. Oh, so soon? Oh, yes. Such efficiency. Very good (*hollow laugh*).

MISS SPELT: It's Deirdre, sir.

MR MAN: Ah, yes. Fine, Deirdre. (*Laughs half-heartedly. He doesn't look at her.*)

MISS SPELT: Are you all right, sir?

MR MAN: Yes, fine . . . yes. (*Realising an explanation is called for.*) Well, actually, no. I'm not feeling up to normal standard. About lunch – perhaps tomorrow?

MISS SPELT: (*worried*) Yes . . .

MR MAN: Busy day. Lots of work. Cancel all my engagements for this afternoon. (*Almost to himself.*) I need some

time on my own (*searching for
excuses*) er . . . important documents
to sort through.

MISS SPELT: Yes, sir. Very well, sir. (*Attempts to
jolly things along, fails.*) 'Bye! (*Exits
and takes mask off.*)

NARRATOR: Mr Man had to think. Why did he do
it? Why did he have to hide behind
his stupid mask? Come to that, why
did he need any of them? He had one
for every situation. There was one
for the boss.

MR MAN: I'm nothing but a yes-man. (*Throws
grovelling mask into the wastepaper
basket.*)

NARRATOR: One to make Scum feel small.
(*Throws red mask into the bin.*) One
to soothe his ego.

MR MAN: (*disgusted*) Do I really look like that?
(*Throws green mask into the bin.*)

NARRATOR: The Monday morning mask.

MR MAN: I've let them take over. I don't need
them. I hate them. But then again
. . . perhaps I can keep just one . . .
just in case . . . what if? . . . no! (*He
drops the miserable mask in slowly.*)
There. Good. (*Sits.*) Right.
(*Uncertain.*) Yes . . .
(NARRATOR *makes telephone noise.* MR
MAN *goes to the phone to answer.
Pauses. Realises he doesn't have a
mask on. Grabs the wastebin and tips
masks all over the floor. He searches
for the right one frantically.*)
Wait a minute! Wait a minute. (*He is
kneeling with a mask half on. He
reaches for the phone but it stops.
Pause.*) What *am* I doing?

NARRATOR: It was a lovely idea while it lasted. But perhaps he could never get rid of them. He picked them up, packed them in his briefcase, put on his 'I've had a hard day at work' mask and set off for home. On his way to the station he started to think perhaps he didn't have the right mask on. It didn't seem to fit properly. But . . . Yes, it was the right one. He arrived at the station just in time to catch his train. He climbed on, the train set off. He looked around at the people who were there every Monday evening.

MR MAN: I wonder, do they all have faces? (*Realises he has unintentionally said this out loud.*) Just clearing my throat.

NARRATOR: At that moment, to his great relief the train stopped. Further down the carriage several people climbed on. The train set off. Mr Man felt most uncomfortable. He had that feeling you get when you think that someone is looking at you – from behind. Could it be? (MR MAN *looks quickly round, just in case.*) Ridiculous. Not a dustbin in sight. The train stopped. Mr Man climbed out of the train. The longer he wore the mask the more uncomfortable it became. Must be his imagination. (MR MAN *is becoming more agitated.*) He just had to take it off. But what would people think?

MR MAN: Let them think! (*He takes it off to his great relief, sees something then hurriedly puts it back on.*) Hello,

Matthew. Have a good day at work?
Neither did I . . . (*sigh of relief*) That
was a close one!

NARRATOR: By the time he was nearly home, the
mask had become unbearable. But
what would his wife say if he walked
in without a mask?

MR MAN: (*determined*) No, I'm going to do it.
(*Takes off mask and puts it in the
case, greatly relieved.*) Yes, that's
better.

NARRATOR: He walked in the door, sat down in
the living room. Read his newspaper
and waited for his wife. (*Puts* WIFE
mask on.)

WIFE: Had a hard day at work, dear? (MR
MAN *quickly hides face behind
newspaper.*)

MR MAN: It's been a terrible day.

WIFE: (*as if not listening*) Slippers?

MR MAN: I didn't get the promotion.

WIFE: Like a cup of tea?

MR MAN: (*nervous*) I lost my temper with my
friend Scum.

WIFE: I got all the washing done.

MR MAN: (*blurts it out*) And I pushed a man
out of the window!

WIFE: Dinner's in the oven.

MR MAN: And, darling . . .

WIFE: (*shocked at his use of a term of
endearment*) Pardon?

MR MAN: Darling (*he lowers the paper.* WIFE *is
taken aback. He stands.*) I've realised
that I've treated you very badly – I've
been living behind a mask all these
years, I don't talk to you any more, I
don't listen to you. There are so
many things I need to tell you. (*With*

difficulty.) Two weeks ago when I said we couldn't afford a new washing machine I went out and bought myself a car radio. I'm sorry.

WIFE: (*dumbstruck, cries, raises mask, to half off, wipes eyes. She sits*) I don't know what's come over you.

MR MAN: I met a man today. He didn't wear a mask. I realised you didn't have to; wear a mask I mean. I want to be like him. I'm going to get rid of them, every single one.
(*Grabs the case and takes the pile of masks out.*)

WIFE: (*putting the mask back on she tries to act as if nothing has happened but is obviously distressed*) Peas . . . peas? Carrots? Dinner won't be long. I must see to the potatoes! (*Exit to* NARRATOR *position keeping mask on but with back to the audience.*)

MR MAN: (*new determination*) I've got to see the boss. I'll speak to Johnson and I'll apologise to Scum. (*Realising what he is saying.*) I'm going to be different from now on. (*Pause.*) I can't do it. I can't do it on my own. If only that man was here. But he's dead. Or is he? (DUSTMAN *enters through audience.*) Perhaps I could talk to him. Perhaps he'd still take them away. Perhaps he'd still want me. I'll go and look for him. (*Sees* DUSTMAN *who is* DSC *with the bin on the floor in front of him.*) Hello. (*Pause.*) I'm glad you are here. (*He holds masks out to him. They look at each other.*)

WIFE: *(entering)* Dinner's ready! *(Sees* DUSTMAN.*)* Oh!
(Brief freeze.)

NOTES ON MAKING MASKS

The success of *About Face* depends not only on a lot of conscientious rehearsal but also on the use of mime and masks.

Mime

It is a good idea for all three actors and director together to explore all the various mimed actions required: e.g. opening curtains, drawers, walking downstairs, handling knives and forks, showing the movement and interior of a train and so on. Much can be achieved by working closely together, paying attention to details. It is always a good idea, and is good fun too, to see if others can guess not only what you are miming but how you are miming it. (See 'Steps of Faith' page 41, by G. & J. Stevenson). Practise as well in front of a large mirror or even use a video recording of yourselves at work – you will soon discover what looks convincing. (It is also a good idea to find out if there are any local evening classes or short courses on mime in your area).

Masks

Half masks which cover all but the mouth and chin are the most practical for this play. There are several techniques when it comes to making masks, and practical books may be found at your library. (See Bibliography). But a simple method we would recommend uses plasticine and papier maché and takes only a few days.

Method:

i) Draw a full size design of the mask you require in profile and front view. Note the measurements of the actor's face, i.e. width from ear to ear across the front, top of forehead to top lip. Note the curvatures.

ii) Prepare a bucket of wall paper paste and tear strips of newspaper (approximately 2 cm by 5 cm).

iii) Take the plasticine – you need approximately 2 kilos per mask (you could use clay), and make a rough face shape on a flat board using the actor's measurements. Using balls of plasticine about the size of a plum start to build up the shape of the actor's features bit by bit, constantly checking the measurements. (A common error is to make the whole thing too flat. Check the depth from ears to nose).

iv) When you are satisfied that you have re-created the rough dimensions of your model, coat it with petroleum jelly (Vaseline) but not too thickly. (This will help ease the finished mask from the mould). Take the torn strips of newspaper and one by one dip them in the paste and lay them on the mould overlapping in different directions to form a lattice work. Smooth out the paper on the mould as you go along, allowing strips to overlap onto the board beneath. Cover the mould twice.

Refer back to your design and start to build up the new features, (nose, wrinkles, etc.) using small sausage-shaped wodges of newspaper and paste. Attach every feature firmly with more strips, building them to the desired proportions. Make sure the whole mask also receives extra layers as you build features. Keep a count of the number of layers; seven or eight should be enough. *NEVER ALLOW THE MASK TO DRY OUT BETWEEN LAYERS*.

If you want to leave it overnight, for example, cover it with a plastic bag.

(An alternative to creating the mask features with papier maché is to actually sculpt the plasticine itself into the desired form. This takes a lot more skill because the dimensions must remain correct, to fit the actor, but it only requires four or five layers of papier maché and will dry out quicker).

v) Leave the mask to dry out in a fairly warm place (not the oven!). This should take up to 36 hours. Remove the mask carefully from the mould and thoroughly wipe the Vaseline off the inside. Wipe the plasticine clean as well. It can then be remoulded for the next mask.

Using strong scissors and a craft knife trim down the edges and cut out the eye shapes (not pin-prick holes but the whole eyeball area between top and bottom lids). The actor should hold the mask to his/her face to determine where it should be cut down. Ensure the nose section does not obstruct mouth movements and that the edges stop short of the ears by 2 or 3 centimetres. The top should be cut to cover the forehead but still allow the hair-line to be seen (in fact if the actor has a fringe the effectiveness of the mask is increased if the hair falls slightly over it at the top).

Make a hole either side of the mask at eye level at least one centimetre from the edge and thread black shirring elastic through, knotting one end inside and adjusting the other as the actor tries the mask on for comfort. Remove elastic ready for painting.

vi) Referring to your design, paint the mask ensuring that hollows receive dark shades and nose, cheeks and forehead, etc. lighter shades. Avoid lines wherever possible, the light source on stage will pick out the contours of the mask. The angry mask may need a more exaggerated treatment, e.g. the whole thing could be painted in shades of red. The jealous mask

could be green. All others should be fairly naturalistic with a slight hint of something different: the
miserable mask could be wrinkled and pallid, the
leering, cheerful mask could have red cheeks,
the secretary's mask with obvious make-up, etc.
The insides should be painted black. Allow to
dry.

vii) Paint p.v.a. (often marketed as children's glue) on
both sides of the mask twice, allowing each coat to
dry before applying the next. Although white when
first applied the glue will dry with a transparent,
almost glossy finish and will give essential protection
and flexibility to the mask. Refit the elastic.

Mask Work

Time should be given to working with the masks before
rehearsals with the script begin. A very simple technique
involves using mirrors. Actors should look at themselves
putting masks on and see what sort of character is suggested. The mask soon dictates a physical response and
work in this area should be encouraged by the director.
Your group could even use the masks for a series of
improvisations to help stimulate their imaginations. Subject matter need bear no relation to the play, in fact new
ideas may develop from your experimentation into per-
formable material of your own, e.g. the plagues of Egypt
represented by masked figures in a dance/drama about the
release of the Israelites or masked actors representing the
hypocrisy of the Pharisees, etc.

Time needs to be given to practising the actual putting on
and taking off of the masks, as the audience should be
aware of a change of physical attitude in the whole body
when this occurs. Such transitions will help convey the
themes of self-deception and fear. It is a good idea for each
actor, and the director, to take turns wearing all the masks
so that everyone has the opportunity to see different inter-

pretations emerging through the improvisations. As with mime, it is observation as well as practice that will benefit the actors and therefore the play.

BIBLIOGRAPHY

Chester J. Alkema, *Mask Making* (Sterling Pub. Inc., USA).

Clive Barker, *Theatre Games* (Eyre Methuen, London).

John Hodgson & Ernest Richards, *Improvisation* (Eyre Methuen, London).

Gordon & Ronni Lamont, *Move Yourselves* (Bible Society, Swindon).

G. C. Payne, *Making Masks* (Pelham Books, London).

G. & J. Stevenson, *Steps of Faith* (Kingsway Pubns, Eastbourne).

Steve & Janet Stickley & Jim Belben, *Using the Bible in Drama* (Bible Society, Swindon).